The Emergence

A Time of Accelerated Change

Howard A. Cooper

BALBOA.
PRESS

A DIVISION OF HAY HOUSE

Balboa Press books may be ordered through booksellers or by contacting:

Balboa Press
A Division of Hay House
1663 Liberty Drive
Bloomington, IN 47403
www.balboapress.com
1 (877) 407-4847

Because of the dynamic nature of the Internet, any web addresses or links contained in this book may have changed since publication and may no longer be valid. The views expressed in this work are solely those of the author and do not necessarily reflect the views of the publisher, and the publisher hereby disclaims any responsibility for them.

The author of this book does not dispense medical advice or prescribe the use of any technique as a form of treatment for physical, emotional, or medical problems without the advice of a physician, either directly or indirectly. The intent of the author is only to offer information of a general nature to help you in your quest for emotional and spiritual well-being. In the event you use any of the information in this book for yourself, which is your constitutional right, the author and the publisher assume no responsibility for your actions.

Any people depicted in stock imagery provided by Thinkstock are models, and such images are being used for illustrative purposes only.
Certain stock imagery © Thinkstock.

Print information available on the last page.

ISBN: 978-1-5043-9537-3 (sc)
ISBN: 978-1-5043-9536-6 (hc)
ISBN: 978-1-5043-9535-9 (e)

Library of Congress Control Number: 2018900547

Balboa Press rev. date: 01/19/2018

This book is dedicated
to Truth
not as we know truth
but as Truth
knows us.

Contents

Preface

This book is about a change in consciousness. It's about changing beliefs and ideals that have been focused on duality and separation. It came about because of a celestial event that I received intuitively as a series of images and insights. This led to a vision that we are in a labyrinth of our own making. This labyrinth has taken us through twists and turns that allowed us to express ourselves in roles that fit the patterns of reality we choose to experience. This journey has been recorded by time and space, and we have accepted its role as reality.

The one constant in time is change. Because of the celestial event I experienced, my insight is that we can take a step in a different direction. In effect, we can emerge from the path we have accepted and choose to realize through knowledge and awareness that we can elevate our consciousness. This book is a beginning in that regard. It is a start that attempts to shine a light down the entrance of our labyrinth so that we may emerge into the ray of a new day and realize the potential of the gifts we have been given.

As we travel along this path of time, people come and go in our lives. Some relationships last for a short period of just an hour, and others last a lifetime. There are some who have helped in one way or another to bring this material to print. Cherlyn Fields, author of *Place 33*, helped us put together the information, website, and YouTube videos for *The Reveal Transit*. Her help was monumental in getting that information out and setting up the website. Barbara

Colgan, who is one of God's angels on Earth, has supported us on trips to sacred sites and in a myriad of discussions and adventures over the years. Judith Schoenthal has supported us in ways untold. Her heart and love of people have no bounds. Gary Rugg, who created the cover of this book, is an amazing graphic artist. For me, there is one person who has supported me through the good and challenging times of my life. She is God's gift for which I am eternally grateful: my wife, Peggy.

This book is a knock on the door of consciousness. Its intent is to bring in a ray of light of knowledge and awareness to the labyrinth of our creations. It asks that we realize that we are a creative expression of a greater whole. Our potential lies beyond what we think our capabilities are, if we allow ourselves the opportunity to know truth.

Introduction

The Emergence
A Time of Accelerated Change

What is the Emergence?

The Emergence is the beginning of a change in consciousness for life on Earth. It is the start of a new way of perceiving what life is and how it's lived. The change starts with the realization that our beliefs are based on a false reality that impairs our ability to identify with our true sense of self and our true purpose in life. The Emergence is a release of the old world of self-identification and the emergence of consciousness that elevates our beliefs in life and the gifts we are blessed with. In reality, it is what comes next.

What comes next? Surrounding us is a combination of destructive tendencies and heartfelt actions and reactions. On the one hand, the world we currently live in moves at a startling pace, and on the other, it seems to retain old concepts of life. We move forward with technology but retain the familiar aspects of life and habits we are comfortable with. The question is this: What is our future if we adhere to our present view of life? What is the future of our children and this planet if we stay on the course before us? The answer can be viewed both optimistically and pessimistically. The future is an opportunity to grow or to destroy what sustains us.

It is more complicated than that, but that realization is a start in a direction of thought.

This thought goes as follows: we are at a gigantic crossroads of existence. We are at the point of an opportunity. We can continue our current conscious stream, or we can look at this moment and realize that certain aspects of our creative collective are not conducive to the creation of a harmonious way of life. No religion, concept of identity, or focus on our life's path is leading us in the direction of an abundant life for all. Why? The reason is not something I can totally explain at this time. It is due in part to our acceptance of a world that believes in lack and limitation for some and abundance for others. We have been at this game of life for eons of recorded and unrecorded time. The elders of the First Nation say, "We have been here before, and this is the fourth world," meaning we have had prior chances without good results. At least that is our impression based on existing conditions.

What is missing? Do our egos present us with such a dilemma that we cannot overcome their influence? Can we not see the truth because we are clothed in human skin and bones of different sizes, shapes, and colors? Are we blinded by the dogma that life is for the survival of the fittest? Is it the karma of cause and effect that keeps us bound by our own actions? Or is it something else—something that appears obvious to wise and holy men, women, and children? What is that something?

I think we have lost our true identity. I think the energies and knowledge associated with truth have been covered in layers of darkness and ignorance. We are not told the truth, nor do we expect to be taught the truth. The energies of mankind have created over time a disconnect from our core and spark of creation. The covenant of creation we have with our Source seems to have been lost. We look for the external, when the truth of our creation lies within. This is why I think we are at a crossroads. We can continue this pursuit of all we currently know and believe, or we can look again at the reason for our being. We can look at something different.

The Emergence is a chance to change our conscious approach to what comes next. It is not an easy solution; if it were, I believe it would have been done a long time ago. This is a time like no other. Maybe we are at a point when men, women, and children are at a stage of consciousness where they are open to making themselves available to a change of perception, an alteration of prior beliefs that no longer serve their greater good.

The way forward is paved with our good intentions. We are at a place of existence where the light of being and the light of our defined self must join together to create an environment where choices are based on a consciousness that seeks harmony and unity, not just with a select few but with the Mind of Creation that we all exist in. This direction appears upward, but in reality, it is within our true nature as part of the totality of existence.

We are part of something that gave us life. It is time in this space and place to realize that the truth of our existence is not just a gift; it is *the* gift. What we do with it is ours and has been ours for eons. The time to realize this is now, and the question is, what do we do about it? The answer lies within the embodiment of your existence. The path you choose is based on the labyrinth you have chosen to tread.

This material utilizes the labyrinth as a road map of your relationship to life. You can see your labyrinth on the earth, in your imagination, or in the heavens above. Or you can see it in all three places based on your focus in life. Again, the choice is yours. The way of the future is yours to choose. We cannot tell anyone what path to choose or make a prediction as to what his or her outcome will be. The law of cause and effect is part of our journey, and the filters we use in life are quite varied—so much so that we cannot predict the results or impact of anyone's journey. All we can do is provide material for each person to consider. If it does not resonate, we urge you to take another path—one you feel will provide you with the results you intuit for your highest good.

I received this information at different times and in a variety of ways. I have pieced this material together in a way that I feel flows with its overall intent. It is not something one should expect to read as if it were a novel. Because of the use of the labyrinth, some of the material seems to repeat itself as if we were walking the circuitous path of a labyrinth. My sense is that some of these subjects require repetition as a form of reinforcement. Change is not an easy subject for many of us. We require some form of stimulant to make it happen. In the change management sessions I attended while still in business, the speakers would say that a business had to create a sense of urgency to institute change within its culture. I don't see this material as creating a sense of urgency as much as a sense of awareness. This material is being presented at this time because there is a need for us to be aware of what is taking place. It will provide us with a foundation of knowledge to move forward with a sense of purpose and overriding intent. This material is not presented to warn of dire circumstances. It is intended to create awareness.

The information in this book is not meant as a quick fix. We have been at the game of life for a long time. Our evolution is one not of minutes but of eons. Our future journey is based on an understanding that it is time to grow as citizens of not only a planet but also a universe. Information requires the willingness to have an open mind and a desire to be more than just your present self. The material in this book is presented at several levels of understanding and experience. When one undertakes an exercise, he or she will find that it provides one result the first time and, with repeated efforts, greater understanding. Not everyone will receive the same results or benefit. This is the truth of those who walk the path. Each person is an expression of the diversity of life. Give to life what you hope to receive from it. Diversity is the fullness of creation.

This material was written because of an event that took place in December 2016. I will go into the details in the opening section of this book. The following sections go into what I feel is needed for humans to awaken to this new and vibrant energy that we are part of. The final section discusses a vision I have of man's potential destiny. Because I realize that science has not discovered the event that started this journey, I have included a list in appendix D of celestial and Earth-related items that cannot be explained based on our current level of knowledge and understanding, if for no other reason than to demonstrate that there are quite a few things we are currently unaware of or cannot explain based on our current scientific knowledge.

This material is presented with the hope and prayer that it will reach those who realize a change in our perception and beliefs in life is required if we are to reach the potential that our Creator has blessed us with.

Peace, for at some level of understanding, we are Light.

Section 1

The Happening

How It All Began

In 2015, I retired after more than forty years as a senior financial and operations executive. Not being one to go fishing, I started to put together some material on a book concept about the potential that exists in all of us. I had worked for and with several companies over the years to help them prosper and grow in productive ways. I always tried to create an environment in which integrity and the growth and morale of the employees were integral parts of the company culture.

In the early part of 2016—I am not exactly sure of the date—I received the impression that there was a wave of some type headed toward Earth. I have had several experiences in my lifetime with mystical events, so I did not react negatively to this experience. I saw it as an enormous wave of what appeared to be energy of some sort. I made a rough sketch of what I saw and put it away.

About a month after that, I saw the same wave, only this time, it appeared larger; it seemed to be much larger than Earth. I made some rudimentary sketches as it appeared to me in relation to Earth. Because I did not have a clue what this meant, I put the drawings in a folder.

In the early part of December, I was half asleep at about three o'clock in the morning, when I suddenly heard the words "Leo and Cygnus." I was immediately wide awake. *What the heck are Leo and Cygnus?* I thought. Then I remembered both were constellations. Although I have had a few psychic experiences, hearing a message in the middle of the night was not something I had experienced before. After about an hour of thinking about what I had heard, I finally fell back to sleep.

That morning, I went to the few books I have on the constellations and looked up both Leo and Cygnus. I am not that knowledgeable about astronomy or astrology, and I did not understand or see a connection between the two constellations. I certainly did not understand what I was to do with what I had heard. I should also mention that when this happened, I did not connect what I heard with the impressions I had received several months prior. I did some research on both constellations and could not find any direct connection between them. We were getting ready for the holidays and did not have a clue why I'd heard the names of the two constellations. My instincts told me something was about to happen.

As the holidays approached, I suddenly had the sense that there was a gigantic wave headed toward our solar system. I checked several scientific websites and could not find anything about this wave. I checked several metaphysical and spiritual websites and found nothing. I could not understand why no one was talking about this event.

I don't remember the exact moment, but it suddenly seemed as if something like a starburst or act of energy had taken place somewhere in the constellation of Cygnus. I could feel the intensity of it, but I was not sure of its power. I was sure this was why I had heard "Leo and Cygnus," but why was I getting this information? I did not understand. I woke up one morning with the sudden realization that the impact of the energy wave was going to be experienced by Earth and our solar system beginning on December 22, 2016, and because of its magnitude, it would last through December 28. It seemed to me to be like a new star in the sky, and it reminded me of the story related to the star of Bethlehem, since it was taking place over the Christmas holiday.

I felt that I had to write about what was taking place. I started to write about it, and without having a complete understanding of what was taking place, I called the event the Reveal Transit because of the impact I felt it would have on us. I based this on my initial impressions of what was about to take place. As I was writing my initial thoughts, it became apparent that I needed to address each day of the event differently. I wrote eight steps, or exercises, that I felt we should do through the course of the event, and I called them the Seven Days of Transitional Awareness. The additional step took place on Christmas Eve.

With only a few days to go before the event, a close friend, Cherlyn Fields, my wife, and I quickly put together a website and created five videos to inform people about what was about to take place. Because of the time frame and the fact that my wife and I had never done this type of thing before, the information did not get out as we had hoped. We did post five videos on YouTube and posted the instructions for the Seven Days of Transitional Awareness on our hurriedly created website: SacredWorldDynamics.com. We then contacted a few friends and our family and shared the information as quickly as we could.

What I received prior to and during the course of the event indicated that this would have a significant impact on the planet Earth, the moon, and our sun. The effect would be experienced throughout our solar system and beyond. My vision and experience were to focus on our sun, the moon, and Earth. I received the knowledge that it was a singular event, something that had never been experienced in our solar system before. The constellation of Leo was involved but on a different level than Earth.

What I realized was that this event would be part of an evolutionary process that we as human beings were going to go through. My sense was that no one would be excluded from this process. The energetic impact seemed to center upon our beliefs and our acceptance of the beliefs that we currently held about this planet and our place on it. The way I described it at the time was that it was similar to an x-ray of a body, in which you see just the bones and an outline. But this was an illumination of our thoughts and beliefs. This is what I wrote in *The Reveal Transit*.

The impact of this radiance would reveal certain facts about our beliefs in self and in one another. It would be like seeing an x-ray of oneself, only it would reveal the contents of one's beliefs and not the physical nature of the self.

I saw it as a chance for us to look at how we functioned in the world and with one another. Since that time, I have tried to gain a greater understanding as to what took place. In doing so, it has come to me that this is a chance to provide some clarity regarding the change that is taking place in the course of humankind's destiny.

I use the term *x-ray*, but this energy is not an x-ray as we know it. I am using my limited knowledge of this energy to describe what took place and the energy that I feel passed through our solar system.

Before continuing, I would like to share an additional vision that I had prior to December 22. I saw an image related to the constellation Leo. It was of a sphinx that was still on its hind legs but was in the process of rising up onto its front legs. Its chest was pointed directly toward the radiance of immense energy from Cygnus. As the image continued, I saw the energy enter and illuminate the heart of the sphinx. Within moments, the illumination moved up toward the head, and it too became illuminated. At the time, I did not fully understand the message associated with this vision, but I knew it was of paramount importance to what was taking place here on Earth and throughout our solar system.

I was not sure why I saw a sphinx as a representation of Leo, but the sphinx has always meant something of great importance to me. The sphinx has always been a symbol for the guardians of the secret places on Earth and sacred knowledge. Because of my research related to trips we have taken to Egypt, I've learned the sphinx has also been connected with the initiation rites in the ancient temples and mystery schools.

In *The Noble Eightfold Path*, Manly P. Hall states, "Lions as part of the cat family have the power of seeing in the dark, and they represent the spiritual sight which is capable of seeing in the darkness of the lower worlds." The lion also stood for courage. Both Buddha and Christ were known as lions for their courage. In other texts, I found that the sphinx stood for royal power and was a symbol for good. Whatever the prior symbolism, the rising and illumination of a sphinx as represented by Leo in my vision has something to do with our ability to see into the darkness we have been accustomed to, and there is a need for us to be courageous as we move forward through the transition before us.

During the writing of this material, I realized that the sphinx, with the body of a lion and the head of a man, is a representation from the celestial realms. We are being asked to have the courage of a lion as we shift our minds from our current state of awareness and evolve in consciousness. In my vision, the illumination started in the heart and went to the head. The connection between heart and mind is the basis for what our future holds.

After December 28, 2016, I felt that whatever was to take place as a result of the event would flow naturally. I was somewhat disappointed in the limited response to the videos and in our ability to get the information out in a timely manner. I knew we had done the best we could in such a short period of time. I was curious to see what would happen next. I did not have long to wait. A few weeks later, again during the middle of the night, I heard clearly, "Tápu'at," followed by "Land of the Rising Sun." I was immediately wide awake. What was the importance of a word that I knew meant a Hopi labyrinth? At least that was what I thought I knew. That morning, I went to search for books I have on labyrinths. Years ago, my wife and I were members of the Labyrinth Society, and we had designed and made a thirty-by-thirty-foot canvas labyrinth based on the Chartres Labyrinth, so I felt I had some knowledge about labyrinths. What I found in *Book of the Hopi* by Frank Waters was not what I'd expected. The heading of the page on T'apu'at design was "Commentary: The Symbol of the Emergence." I stared at the page for several minutes as I tried to grasp what that meant. I began to realize that we were in a time of transition that would take us to a whole new concept of reality.

The information in this book has come to me like a gigantic jigsaw puzzle. I thought at first I would write a small booklet on this material. As I started to write, the information I was receiving just kept coming. I believe I have somehow tapped into the Infinite Mind of Creation to write this material. Sometimes the sentence structure is not what we think of as proper English, but I have tried to make few changes to what I received. I placed the material in a sequence that I feel is logical. Not everything I received is logical, but I have faith in its validity. As I stated earlier, some of the material seems to go back over itself as if walking through the path of a labyrinth.

The challenge for me has been to write this material and then work with it in an effort to gain a greater level of awareness and understanding. Because I have accepted the concepts and beliefs of the third-dimension prior to becoming aware of this information and knowledge, I have an understanding of what it takes to benefit from this material. It has allowed me to gain insight that has enhanced my outlook on life.

During the course of writing this material, I received a vision that is different from those who predict the end of days or an apocalypse. It does speak to the fact that if we want a future different from what we are experiencing today, we have to change our beliefs in separation, duality, and impermanence.

Transition from the Reveal
Transit to the Emergence

As the Reveal Transit energy left our space in the solar system, it left behind a change in what we perceive as our reality. The impact was not felt like a strong wind but more like a gentle breeze. If you are not aware, it seems to pass unnoticed. The reality is that what took place has changed many things throughout the planetary logos. The vibration of change we are currently experiencing and will experience is more dynamic and, in some ways, more chaotic. After the event passed, I seemed to lose the initial intensity I had felt. At first, I questioned if it really happened or if it was an illusion. As I watched world events unfold, I began to see greater extremes play out across our world, and I wondered if this was due in part to what had just taken place. I came to the conclusion that it was humanity responding to the nature of what had already been set in motion over eons.

After a short period of time, it became apparent that the vision and feelings I had were not something I could dismiss. I had to start writing about the impact of this event and what was taking place within the essence of our beings. It was ironic that I had started to write about potential in my earlier material, and now I was to write about potential in a way I'd never imaged. When I sat down to write the first piece of material, it became apparent that this subject was much more involved and wider in scope than I had initially perceived. It was as if I were tapping into a stream of consciousness that had its own way of communicating thoughts and knowledge. After a while, I felt I was communicating with the Infinite Mind of Creation, where knowledge and wisdom are expressed at a different level of consciousness.

The Emergence from our present state of awareness to the next step in our evolution is not something mankind pays much attention to. We are caught up in the day-to-day aspects of our lives. For many, just getting through the day is a challenge. For others, pleasures of the material world occupy their time. There have always been a handful of souls who choose to follow the spiritual path and seek greater understanding of self and the universe. The level of awareness that is currently present on Earth follows a rather narrow range. The motivation to know the next step is somewhat blinded by our current thoughts and beliefs. The realm of third-dimensional reality is fixed on the dramas we have created and our investment in them. From what I understand from this material, it is time for us to realize some greater truths.

The Cygnus event brought to my attention the labyrinth of the Hopis that they called Tápu'at. I knew about the labyrinth, but I was not aware of its meaning. A labyrinth is not only important to our human psyche and spirit but also a way for us to symbolize our journey through life. The fact that the symbol of the Hopi labyrinth meant the Emergence was like a lightbulb going off in my head. We were going to travel a route that led in some way to our emergence into a new level of consciousness. The question I had was this: How? The following information is thus a small step in that direction. You will note that there are two or three different writing styles. Please have patience with some of the information as written. I have tried not to change too much of what I received.

So It Begins

What took place during the Reveal Transit brought a subtle shift in human consciousness and human interaction. Appearance of a continuance in the drama and platform of life appears normal. The foundation for existence appears the same. Old habits of existing norms move or appear to move in a sequence that seems normal. The truth is that the foundation of fundamental relationships has been altered. This is a result of the celestial event of 2016. The alteration is not only cosmic in nature but also on a microcosmic level, being reflected in relationships. That which is defined as magnetic in form is altered, as is the connection of subatomic particles. Mass moved in a relationship to the influence of energy. The equation of mass to energy is not the same as that of Einstein's theory. Nowhere does man understand the concepts embedded in the movement of mass versus the undifferentiated field of absolutes. Mankind is the surface; the cells are the accumulation of a concept. The movement from cell to surface now is a mystery for those who perceive the fullness of life. Form comes from the formless. How? It is a mystery of life that will be revealed at the appropriate time as we move to higher levels of consciousness. I have written this paragraph as I received it. The change that we are experiencing comes to us in a form that is beyond the concepts and knowledge that we currently know and accept.

The subject at hand is the impact or effect the Reveal Transit has on mankind. This is the story of change. The code exists in light. So what is the impact on life going forward, or is it upward? Night and day follow one another, just as the intent of humanity's flow follows what is perceived as real. The motivation of man is what? The motivation of man is to evolve—conscious, subconscious, and unconscious. The patterns of reality have an inherent sequence. This is like the progression of seasons or the cycles of a universal matrix. All life on Earth seeks, on one level or another, to evolve. The sequence of events over eons appears as a steady progression. This progression has been, when seen from the perspective of the ages, uneven at best. There have been stops, starts, and reversals along the way. There have been ups and downs as seen from the standpoint of evolution.

No individuals leave Earth without an understanding of their progression in the evolution of their state of consciousness and their soul growth. This is a lesson in existence. Now comes an event that was not consciously experienced. It was not consciously experienced because of the capacity of man to accept his status as a celestial citizen. How would we understand an event that was so immense that it interacted with an entire solar system and beyond? How much fear and chaos would develop as a result of something that had never been encountered before? Life as you know it would potentially collapse. That was not meant to happen at that time, so the event went unnoticed by most of mankind and by those in the scientific community.

The current view of existence is changing because of the energies that passed through our realm of experience. There is a set pattern of reality described as "that which is" in esoteric terms. Because we are in this set pattern we expect certain aspects of life to remain in a state that we can identify with. Something that appears normal. The change we are experiencing now will accelerate and "that which is", as a set pattern, will begin to shift and will become more noticeable as we move forward. This is not a beginning or an end of anything other than what conscious belief consists of. This is an opportunity for mankind to take this moment in time and space to realize the potential of the energy that now gives rise to increased use of consciousness and intent. This is a moment of renewal of conscious awareness and the identification of false beliefs. No man is alone in this regard. This is consciousness raising at many levels of existence.

Life is not stationary. The moment of conscious expansion is like a pot of water about to boil. It is intensifying, and the result is a change of nature, a change of material form and content. How this impacts the future remains to be seen, but this opportunity should not go unnoticed. It should be brought to the attention of consciously evolving beings.

Know that mankind takes his turn on the scale of evolution like every other aspect of creation. The scale or level of conscious awareness does not materially matter. What is of importance is the desire to fulfill the possibilities of the time. Space is occupied by intelligence. This is not known for several reasons, which are based in the belief of separation. Identification of other[1] does not allow for the permanence of intelligence in the seeming void of space. The intelligence of the time relieves one of the responsibilities of knowing what is unknowable at present, except for a few advanced souls and incarnates who have progressed the ladder of conscious evolution.

---

[1] See appendix A.

What Are We Emerging From?

Did you know that we are creating history? Our current experience is the dynamic of what will be written, studied, and talked about. What we do today changes the world's concept of itself tomorrow.

Did you know that our ancestors lived through various ages of what we describe as darkness and light? We had the Dark Ages and the Renaissance. These periods of recorded history reflect different stages of man's evolution. Before recorded history, mankind moved around the planet with just enough barely to survive. There are other periods of time when we are not sure exactly what took place, because we lack physical documents and artifacts. We are aware of monuments carved out of stone that indicate mankind possessed knowledge we do not fully understand or are not aware of today. There seem to be gaps between recorded history and what we believe our roots to be.

The timeline of yesterday and today is filled with unknown moments and accurate (we think) documented history. All of this is from our current perspective, which we know has changed over time. Earth is flat, and the sun revolves around Earth—these are just two glaring examples. We believe our ancestors lived initially in a primitive state of survival, and then we made a steady advancement over eons to what we believe is our state of reality today: modern man with our modern, hyper evolving technology. We believe we are educated, and we believe we know where we stand on the stage of evolution.

I have a theory. My theory goes as follows.

Our current state of affairs as a planetary species is currently in an age of darkness. We have been in this age for a lot longer than we are willing to believe. Our current conduct as human beings have little to no understanding of our current state of affairs.

We are held to our convictions by the limited nature of accepted beliefs. Those beliefs include a lack of understanding of our true nature as guardians not only of one another but also of this planet. We have accepted for ages the concept of survival of the fittest. We believe in the inequality of life—that one person or group is better or worse than another for any reason you can conjure up.

We are still in an age of darkness because of our tendency to burn books, manuscripts, and sacred texts and experience the destruction of ancient holy sites in the belief that one group has a better way forward than another. We feel we can and should destroy one another because of our different beliefs, and wars of humanity are a way of life and the way to resolve major differences. Think back to the beginning of recorded time, and then look at today. The only difference is how our wars are fought. Our distribution of wealth and resources is not based on a universal approach; it is based on dominance. This has gone on for eons, and we have accepted this as normal.

Today we are faced with the changing of facts to fit a person's or group's point of view. Did you ever think about the saying "The winners write history"? How much of recorded history has been distorted to reflect the views of the so-called winners? What do we think when we are told that Russia is interfering in America's and France's election processes? This is just another example on an international scale of one group rewriting facts to support their ideology.

How many times do we open a paper, see the evening news, or go on the Internet and cringe at the bloodshed and senseless loss of life? How many times are we asked to accept the fact that we are willing to kill one another for any reason you can think of and maybe no apparent reason at all?

I know some will say, "We now have the Internet and the cloud, so we can get any information we desire. Knowledge is all around us. Schools of higher education can be found throughout the world." This is true, but the point of being in darkness is not what you know; it is what you don't know that makes a difference.

Why are the mysteries of our existence limited to a select few? Why is the color of your skin a factor in anything? Why is there a difference in certain countries of this world in your gender? Why does monetary wealth differentiate one from another? Why is the goal of the world powers to achieve their goals through force or dominance? Why is the bottom line of a company seen as success or failure? Why do we accept pain and suffering as part of life? The list of questions is endless.

The time we accept as now in history leads us to another issue: What comes next? What is the level of our evolution as we move from the physical to the mental form of expression? What happens when artificial intelligence does the work that mankind depends on for his daily activity and sustenance? How do we regroup as individuals when machines can occupy, educate, and entertain our waking hours? What happens to human relationships when technology surrounds us? What is nature when the time of our consciousness is confined to our minds and not our hearts or our instincts? What becomes of Earth when we occupy ourselves with other planets? How do we express more of our true potential as creative beings when technology robs us of our natural abilities? Before you dismiss that question, think about GPS usage and not our natural abilities to go from one place to another. How many different types of drugs are there to alter our reality, and who benefits?

The age of darkness is not the end of the world but an opportunity. This opportunity before us is not the completion of a journey but the continuance of a chance to not only change the possibilities of life but also enhance life. The question is this: How? I don't profess to have all the answers, but I do believe I can open the door just a little to have us look at things differently.

Labyrinth

Here is my vision based on what I perceive is taking place. We as human beings have, for the sake of evolution, entered into the space occupied by the planet we call Earth. This place is part of a dynamic vibrating at a scale that allows for the illusion of separation, duality, and impermanence. We have come to this home as an opportunity to expand our knowledge and demonstrate the freedom of creative expression. We entered this plane of reality with knowledge and wisdom, but as we became more entangled in this vibration and energy, we accepted the basic premise of this world of fragmented reality as real. Instead of being part of the totality of our experience, we choose to be apart from it, separate and disconnected from our inner truth. Instead of directing the lesson, we became the lesson. When we entered the labyrinth of life on Earth, we in effect entered an age of darkness.

The age of darkness is the state of occupied thought and beliefs that came from the will to survive—not in the way of spiritual beings but in the way of the hunters of life and not as cavemen but as separate entities in the shell of human forms. We are the product of an environment that calls for expression by something other than our true essence. Our journey through this labyrinth has been relatively short by cosmic standards but long from the human perspective of time.

In my vision, the entire race of humanity is in a large and somewhat complicated labyrinth. Because we are all unique, each of us treads this labyrinth's path in a distinct way. We are part of a greater whole, but because we see and believe in our uniqueness at the level of ego, we have accepted the belief in the concept of separation at a dense level. In addition, the mass consciousness that is our reality allows us to function at a level of duality we do not fully comprehend or appreciate. The circumstances of our life get lost in the active/reactive mode of existence that we accept as part of existence.

The labyrinth is in fact a path, and it is a path of our choosing. It is the path of accepted reality. As we journey around this labyrinth, we accept the world for what it appears to be. We accept its beliefs, its concepts, and, thus, its seeming reality. Because we are all unique, we see and process the experience of this world with different eyes and interpretations of what life is and how it is lived. This is not a fairy tale, for it holds the seeds of truth. We have all come to experience a labyrinth as part of the conscious and unconscious application of life.

For those not familiar with a labyrinth, I should explain what a labyrinth is. A labyrinth is a complex and circuitous path that leads from a beginning point to a center. Labyrinths have one way in and one way out. They have one path, and that path leads to the center.[2] In an article written in the June 2012 issue of *Theosophy* by John Algeo, regarding *The Theosophical Labyrinth*, he wrote: "Walking a labyrinth by passing from its entrance to its center and then returning back to it circumference thus represents several analogous processes: the coming into birth and the passing out of earthly life of an individual, the involution and evolution of a universe, and-most important-a journey into the center of our own being, the achievement there of a quest for wholeness, and the subsequent return to our divine source".

The physical representation I received is of a Hopi labyrinth. As I stated earlier, this labyrinth came to me as a word one night when I was half asleep. The word was *Tápu'at*, followed by "Land

---

[2] See appendix B which provides more information on labyrinths.

of the Rising Sun." I found that the word is related to the myth of the Emergence based on the Hopi tradition. There are two symbols that supposedly are related: one is a masculine form, and the other is a feminine form. I have chosen the feminine form of the labyrinth, which is known as mother and child. I feel this relates to the birth of consciousness I believe is taking place.

The Land of the Rising Sun signifies the beginning of a new chapter in the evolving consciousness of man. This land is not an island or a continent. It is the face of the landscape man must direct his attention to. The way forward on the journey of mankind is to realize that the rising of the sun indicates beginning. It is a new day in the life and times of what is now accepted as third-dimensional reality. Once the time of change is realized, mankind can lift up his eyes to a new vision of what is possible, not in the present way of perceiving and experiencing his way of life but in a way that is not available when the status quo is accepted.

The Land of the Rising Sun also signifies that the rays of reality that play a part in the nature of things are changing. These rays are like the beams that stream forth from our physical sun. They enhance the nature of things. What is considered enhanced by some may be seen and accepted as less than ideal by others. The journey of man is filled with many aspects of acceptance. How one accepts this message is a sign of his or her current state of consciousness. As will be stated many times throughout this material, there is no judgment in this statement. It's hard for some to believe but is true from a level that understands the progression of man.

Tápu'at

Although the labyrinth appears flat on this paper, in reality, it is anything but. It is a multidimensional experience made up of layers of vibrational frequencies that allow us the full expression of our will to be.

From my perspective, we enter the labyrinth to experience the lessons of the world. There is one way into the labyrinth of life and only one way out. This format differs from a maze, which has several ways in and potentially several ways out. What we encounter in the labyrinth is a matter of choice. How we proceed through the labyrinth depends on the circumstances we encounter along the way. If we choose, we can step off the path, stop along our journey, or even seem to go back over steps we have previously traveled. The path of the labyrinth is filled with our desires, intentions for growth, and life lessons. Each step through the labyrinth is, in effect, the evolving of our being. As we take this journey, we are not alone. We come together with family, friends, and groups who travel with us as we journey through the labyrinth. Our free will allows us the choices we make as we traverse the labyrinth. This labyrinth is shrouded in mystery for most of us because of our focus on the attractions of third-dimensional reality. As time has gone by, more and more souls have evolved beyond this labyrinth and can see it for what it truly is: an illusion.

The laws of cause and effect have allowed mankind the ability to visit and revisit the role of the labyrinth related to the Earth experience over time. Because of the timing of the celestial event and the information I have received, it appears we can move forward at a faster pace in our evolution if we choose.

My vision for the race of man is to move beyond the present confines of our beliefs and accepted ideals. The scope of this endeavor is rather involved, and the degree of difficulty appears not only complex but also monumental. I believe it is time for mankind to elevate his consciousness to a level where we can understand what the freedom of expression truly means and restore our unity with one another and ourselves through the knowledge that we are all sacred. We are an expression of divine creation.

Because of the celestial event that took place in December 2016, I believe we have an opportunity to emerge from the labyrinth to a new way of viewing ourselves and the world. The Emergence is a beginning but at the same time a continuance of a journey we have been on for many eons.

The Emergence from the
Labyrinth of Life

W ho you are changes over the course of a lifetime. The dynamics
of life ebb and flow. The relationships of life appear and then
move on to new and different dynamics. The things of life are born
and then, in the creative consciousness, move in different ways to a
level of completion. The life of the planet moves through the solar
system in the same way but on a different scale within the concepts of
evolution and with differing results over an extended period of time.
Mountains are created and then seem to remain static. The changes
are like waves in the ocean: ever present but difficult to differentiate.
The dynamics are concealed[3] in apparent sight but not fully noticed
or, if noticed, not fully understood.

Now conscious beings have encountered a celestial event that moved
through us and the universe. It requires recognition. The celestial event
was encountered consciously by more than a few sensitive and intuitive
souls. The result of this encounter is an abrasive impact on individual
beliefs. The timing of the event came on the eve of a new sun above the
horizon. The sun was in effect opened by the passing of this celestial

---

[3] My thoughts on concealment are as follows: Concealment is the lack of
understanding or appreciating the foundation of existence—that which is
all around but not seen or realized as existence. People move through the
dynamics of third-dimensional reality as if nothing else existed. Nothing
that is real is concealed from the heart of those who seek truth. Nothing is
more obvious than the truth when it is the only thing in life that is essential.

event. This means Earth's sun has more intensity related to its impact on life. It is also registering a higher vibration and frequency which is causing the human aspect of life to experience different challenges. These include comprehending the term *unity of conscious intent* and the belief in the current mode of reality as real existence. The dynamic of life has a passing impact on conscious awareness, but few who currently exist now have an understanding of true reality when it comes to the truth in galactic and universal terms.

Many have gained self-realization, and some have experienced the release of bodily confinement, but none have witnessed the direct light of an open sun until now. Mankind has been shielded from many celestial events that would have caused major disruption in conscious evolution until now. The open sun[4] is a unique, dynamic experience and opportunity. It is a time of changing perceptions and accepted beliefs. What makes this real is the motion within all of existence. All things are governed by cycles and rhythms. All things in existence are energy in form and content. The world is a result of conscious interpretations of knowns and unknowns. It is a result of mass consciousness taken to levels of manifestation that are accepted as fact. This is absolute in the vibratory field of current and bygone consciousness.

One must wonder what this is all about and ask, "How am I impacted as a human being living my life on Earth at this time?" The first dynamic to be addressed involves the changes brought about by a conscious blueprint embedded in life. This blueprint resides in motion and is an active aspect of evolution. It consists of the motion and vibration of particles that have intelligence and the ability to form relationships. This is akin to energy following thought. There is more to this that falls under the laws of magnetic

---

[4] Open sun: The sunlight that surrounds this planet nurtures life. That sun has been restricted by the limited perception of man. Now, because of the force of the celestial event, the sunlight, with its ability in this reality to nurture life, has been clarified to a certain degree and enhanced. This is the light of a new day. There is more to this than I am privy to at this time.

attraction that needs further exploration. Our innate intelligence is not finite; it is infinite. The only boundaries exhibited are centered on accepted beliefs. This subject is part of a mystery of the third-dimensional existence. When the word *mystery* is used, it means that the key is found in continuing our quest through love—not the love that we think of but a love that is infinite in expression. There is no way to describe it, for it is the foundation of our ability to create. What comes to me is that this is an endless stream that we have the potential to express if we choose to make ourselves available to its call.

The second dynamic is the play of a great intelligence that governs the world in its order. This intelligence has its home in universal thought and universal consciousness. The way to the light of knowledge is through the intelligence that is within the seed of our existence. This too is a mystery for mankind because we dwell in the finite world of individual and group perception.

The way through the current situation is through reflection on the great unknowns of life. It is through the release of agreed-upon norms. That which appears fixed is dynamic. That which is dynamic seeks another level of finite reality. The way to the new is the release of the old. Due to the time and place of this current moment, we have the opportunity to realign consciousness with spirit. This realignment is the essence of becoming as one in emerging from existing states of consciousness. The focus is on unity and not separation.

All of life is in a constant state of change. There is life in the form of either transition and evolution or what appears as decline, a form of decay or devolution. Either way, transition is a form of change. What makes a difference in the life of existing human beings is their intent. The focus of one's intent is linked to his or her belief in the impermanence of life and the rituals associated with life. Age is not a form of decline. Age is the transition from learning the lessons of life to expressing those lessons. No person or thing leaves this plane of existence without adhering to this dictate or law of evolution.

I want to share a personal observation here. This statement about age was startling. I now understood why so many of us become teachers, advisers, and volunteers and do charity work as we get older. I also took it to mean that we needed to stay active and flexible as we age. This is the opposite of what many of us do, and inactivity can contribute to disease and physical and mental issues. Many of us become inflexible as we age, both mentally and physically. We have to find ways to express and utilize the experiences of a lifetime.

Mankind's element of expression is based not on knowledge but on experience. The reflection of people's intent is exhibited by their physical appearance. This is a classification of expression of belief in the known and unknown forces of life. Mankind dwells in isolation because of the unknown quality of his intent, which has become his physical expression. All of life dwells in a sea of beliefs. The acceptance of belief is due to vibratory assimilation of a higher nature. When people accept their status in life, they become the vibration of their acceptance in physical and mental form. They are the appearance of vibration and frequency of belief and what they accept in life. The indwelling nature of their existence only changes when life intrudes into their consciousness. Action and reaction of life are a result of a life lived in the belief that negative and positive experiences are caused by external forces. Now is the moment of realization that beliefs are the center of all existence in the current moment of expression. Cause and effect are the accumulation of accepted beliefs. The time to adhere to a new core of conscious beliefs is here and now as an opportunity of unlimited potential.

The following is a list of what appear to be core issues related to our experiences on Earth and in the third dimension:

- Mankind is the product of isolated thinking in what appears as the vacuum of space.
- Mankind does not consciously realize his link to the divine.
- Mankind and Godkind are linked by a series of issues that have been embedded in conscious and subconscious thought.

- Evolution of humanity appears as a past element of existence.
- The role of man is not seen as a guardian of his home, Earth.
- The relationship between what are deemed heaven and Earth is not understood at a conscious experiential level.
- Walking through life is a form of existence that releases one from responsibility.
- The level of consciousness exhibited creates a level of separation that is accepted as real.
- Mankind dwells in the consciousness of a cloudy environment brought about by the belief in and acceptance of the consciousness term *other*.
- All of life evolves, but the mechanism of evolution is seen as science, not truth of creation.
- "All men are created equal" is not accepted as fact but as a part of an unrealistic concept.
- Only certain aspects of creation can interact and communicate with the will of the divine.

These core issues are with us at birth and through life. They represent our willingness to accept the beliefs of mass consciousness. What happens when one forgets the role that exists within his or her internal acceptance of life before entry into the realm of life we accept as real? That which is forgotten is not only crucial to the expression of the individual spark of life; it is the fundamental reason for being. The association we have to truth of being is temporarily lost or covered over to allow for the part we play in life to manifest. This central core of our being is important for us to remember as we journey down the path of life. Shakespeare said we are all actors on a stage. This is due in part to the illusions associated with this reality, the roles we play, and the way we play them. They conform to the time and place of our entry into life.

The light of awakened thinking is dawning as a subject as it is brought into the conscious stream of man's awareness. Light is a subject of truth. By entering the cave of darkness, light became an afterthought. It became the other side of the awakening of man. Light is not dense, but it is a vehicle of communication. Light is the product of the Creator's energy. Light dwells within man because the Creator's image is in man. This is not hard to believe when consciousness is accepting of wholeness, but it's hard to comprehend from the state of present consciousness. Wholeness is an application of truth. Wholeness is the opposite of nothing. When mankind evolves, so does the conscious acceptance of higher states of awareness. This now is the opportunity to accelerate that level of awareness, which is available to one and all.

If we hold the notion that all of life is the result of coincidence and happenstance, the current state of illusion will persist. Life has a meaning. It is meant to be understood and experienced at a conscious level called truth.

Celestial Event Revisited

All of life is impacted by the real and unreal concepts of one's creations. The life of each and every person is linked by a universal force of creation. It is called by many names, but for the eternal now, it is referred to as One. Lines of force reveal nothing to those who cannot or choose not to see and experience truth. The many aspects of creation are, by definition, force or energy. They are dynamic, and they exist as life exists, moment by moment in a state of constant motion and diverse expression. The Life of the One in which we all reside. (As a side note, I sense that this is referring to a form of intelligence that underlies the matrix of life both seen and unseen.)

Mankind has been visited by the energy of a celestial event that I named the Reveal Transit. This event has a unique dynamic and impact. This event was unique as it applies to life's beliefs. It ignites the mind and emotions to recognize that which no longer provides the assurance that life is as it seems. The focus of beliefs holds patterns of thought and potential of both a constructive and destructive nature. All of mankind has a choice to hold on to what no longer applies as their belief structure, which is illusionary, or go through a process of letting go. The great let go. As far as I can tell, everything was impacted by this event, including Earth, the moon, and the sun. The rising of the sun now signals a new day of completion. Let no man doubt the world has changed. The focus of today is the rising sun. This focus is to reveal the transition that is taking place.

The beliefs we hold on to are of past energies or thought forms that are difficult, if not impossible, to hold on to due to the Reveal Transit—the sticky stuff of false beliefs and acceptance of models of life that are at odds with current energies.

The following is a way of beginning to find alignment with the energies we are currently experiencing as a result of the celestial event we went through in December. The first declaration is acknowledging the light that now flows through the solar system as represented by our sun. The ancient Romans saw December 25 as the beginning of a new sun. On that day in 2016, I felt it was the apex of what was taking place in and around Earth.

Unfoldment

The unfolding of consciousness begins and ends with self. Let me repeat: the unfolding of consciousness begins and ends with self. No one creates the unfoldment of conscious intent without an inner spark of reality being ignited. The life of one being is like a candle being lit in the darkness of space. Nowhere does mankind exist without this spark. The ignition of the desire to achieve is part of the unfoldment. That which is brings forth the energy to allow for transition. The focus of this energy is not personal but universal. The individual relationship to this energy and unfoldment is based on conscious availability. Does a person seek knowledge and growth, or is he or she content with current levels of existence? The individual aligns with the currents of time and either accepts or denies the status quo. The timing and way in which this takes place as a form of change are unique to each individual life force.

That which is now seeks change in the form of recognition. Mankind is about to face a test of his view of life. It is transition at its finest. The unfoldment of consciousness and of intent to release ancient perceptions of reality is going to be tested, not in the form of discord but in the way of a release of knowledge. Let this come to pass through the transmission of words, thoughts, and concepts.

The unfoldment of knowledge is like the opening of a book. It is a release of what is meant to be.

The way of the current moment is an ingredient in what is an evolutionary state of human history. Mankind has taken quantum leaps in the past with varying degrees of what some would classify as limited success. The truth is that evolution is based on the potential embedded in consciousness and in the freedom to create according to cosmic cycles and rhythms. Mankind is part of the cosmic order. People believe in separation because of the limits placed on third-dimensional thought. It is the structure and form of human interaction with life. The existing physical makeup of life justifies the belief in separation. The acceptance of separation thoughts and beliefs in daily existence is taken for granted. It is an accepted norm.

More individuals have taken leadership roles to evolve their consciousness toward the divine. Now, in this moment of evolution, there has come a force of nature to propel mankind in a new, if not obvious, direction. That direction is to live life in a state of knowledge of the finite and the infinite—unity with the true direction of human potential and with the true nature of living things we interact with in life.

The time has come to attempt to understand and use the ways of the ancestors. By yourself, the world is lonely. With others, the world is still lonely. Why? The purpose of man is unity—with self and with the life force that sustains us. Mankind does not understand that life is sacred, because he does not understand the true nature of unity. Most people do not choose the road of understanding because of the nature of their beliefs. They choose the consciousness associated with group dynamics. These dynamics lead one to associate with things, or objects of adoration. They are not bound to anything, because this is isolationist thinking. It is belief in a greater whole that is fragmented. This leads to a universal belief in *I* as an object, not as a creation of the One, the Almighty in Light.

Too many are drawn from the light into darkness due to this acceptance of group consciousness. The light of awareness is whole in stature and in reality. One chooses group over unity to experience belief in other. Other is the classification of separation. Other is something outside the self. Inner vision is clouded by stuff associated with group consciousness. Due to the rhythm and vibration of the time, the disruption of the current plan of accepted beliefs is at hand.

How do you change from false beliefs to live consciously in truth?

The willingness to change has to originate within the consciousness of self. The spark of creation seeks awareness. Within the inner aspect of self lies the truth of the direction in life. People must first realize they have accepted beliefs that are from preexisting consciousness. The first question is this: What do I believe and why?

What is the source of your current beliefs, and how have you grounded them into the makeup of your existence? This is a starting point. More will be discussed in future material.

The reality of life is one of illusion when there is separation of any kind in the mind and the perception of one's existence. Life is illusion in form and in reality when one does not abide in love. The term *love* does not stand for an individual expression; it stands for unity of expression. It is beyond thought and beyond emotion. Love is the dynamic expression of a creative force in which *all* is defined by unity in a consciousness that is complete and whole. The term *love* does not apply to forgiveness of self, for true love is whole without judgment. This may be hard to comprehend, but love is a complete expression of unity. Love that we speak of is beyond the limiting concepts of light and darkness we accept as reality. Love is the balance point of one's awareness.

Oneness is the totality of expression of love without limits or boundaries. All is everything, and everything is an expression of the totality of All There Is. The "small" *I* defines self in the space of third-dimensional thinking and experience. The *I* in universal consciousness is the totality of expression. It is a complete unit of universal consciousness, thought, and application of reality. The secret of secrets is wholeness through love. Unite in oneness now through love is not just a random thought, it is an application of conscious intent that is required now and in the future.

The Six Questions

Because of the nature of the information, I decided to put together six questions in an effort to understand the concepts that I was receiving. As I was writing the answers, I got the impression to write an introduction to each question. The heading that begins the introduction was the first impression I received before I started to write the answer. The information follows the heading and then leads into each question that I asked.

Tápu'at

Tápu'at is that which is to emerge and that which is conscious evolution. It is the state of reality about to open or is in the process of opening. It is to emerge from the darkness of the illusion of false identification.

What Is the Emergence?

Prior knowledge is left behind as the time for change is upon the landscape of Earth and in those who inhabit the sphere of third-dimensional thinking and beliefs. The way to the future is not based on the episodes of the past. It is based on knowledge—the knowledge that lives right below the consciousness of everyday thinking and is above the horizon of man's current acceptance of life's continuum. The way of future thought and ideals is through the simplicity of desire, the open door of faith in the truth. One by one, many will allow time and space the room to become aware of what true potential is and why it is so important to the evolution of man.

The will to emerge from existing states of consciousness is seen for what it is: a way forward. The emergence of mankind's creativity to produce at a higher level of what is considered acceptance is readily available. The way to new thought is to realize that there is a necessity to seek the higher realms of what exists within. The way forward is a focus on the realization that mankind is part of a process of evolution. This is the moment to realize the impact of creativity when it is directed toward a higher goal. That goal is to open to the inner aspects of truth and, in the process, reveal the innate talents of a creative whole. As a side note, this seems to refer to a level of consciousness that is more unified and aware than what we currently use.

The time of emergence from the darkness of existing norms is at hand. The union of man, stars, and the cosmos is only a breath away. The knowledge of the light associated with the emergence awaits no one, for it is here in this current moment. Open the heart, and reveal the true dimensions of what is real. This is done through a realignment of thoughts and ideals. The universe seems to be full of complexity, but truth reveals itself for what it is when desire, belief, and faith are aligned in proper order.

Wake this morning to a new light. This light provides the illumination to reveal the existence of a labyrinth of thought and experience. The entrance to this labyrinth was at birth, the beginning of a journey. Mark the time of entrance as a test of one's purpose to create in the greater aspect of creation. Mark the time as birth of a desire to move the energies of life as a co-creator with the Light of Lights. The entrance was a beginning, and the journey has been seemingly full of twists and turns. Creation's energy was used for what seemed both good and bad. Life seems to swing to full at times and empty at other times. The way was filled with joy, sorrow, love, and hate. Successes were many, and there were losses too. The journey turned in many ways, and with the turns came a sense of darkness and the loss of memory for the purpose and gifts of creation. The loss can be seen as a form of darkness, and in some quarters, it is termed ignorance, not in a demeaning way but as the result of ignoring your greater truth.

The light of existence now shines on a new direction. That direction is straight down the opening of the entrance of your labyrinth. It is the sunrise of a new opportunity to awaken to a greater truth; that truth not only exists in each of us but also flows from the Mind of Creation. It is time for the Emergence from darkness to be revealed. The subject of what follows lines up with this opportunity. Let no man awaken unprepared for this event. Time and space are available. So is the energy of knowledge. Let's begin.

Leo and Cygnus

The constellations move in the heavens. They move to the rhythm of all life that moves in us. The organization of stars has meaning in their progression and impacts us because we are part of something much greater than we currently realize. The movement of stars is not fixed but changes as we go through the progression (as we see it) of life.

Why Is There a Change in Consciousness at This Time?

The rotation of life in the firmament is enhanced by the events of creation and seeming destruction. Planets, stars, suns, galaxies, and universes evolve. What's in one place in the universe of creation impacts, to one degree or another, other aspects of life. The level of impact is not universal in that not all aspects of planetary existence expand and contract at the same frequency. All is diverse in the multiple spectrums of reality. Thus, expansion and contraction are not universal.

The timeline of expansion in this realm of reality took a jump, if you will. The impact of the creation in space was felt throughout the horizons that mankind inhabits. This creation of a force of dynamic energy came to Earth in the form of what I will call starlight. The exact composition of this energy will be revealed when mankind's consciousness will accept and comprehend it.

The focus of the energy was felt at levels of consciousness that were not apparent at the time it intercepted Earth. The important point of this information is to reveal its impact not in the physical realm but in the realm of conscious and subconscious patterns— in effect, the basis of beliefs. This is new to conscious awareness. The impact of energy patterns of consciousness is not new, but the impact of this type of energy intercepted by Earth and its inhabitants is a change from normal streams of consciousness. The highlighting of beliefs is a strange occurrence from normal progressions of life.

The Leo-Cygnus relationship is apparent to those who seek its deeper interpretation. The highlight of this connection is through the portals of mind. That which is (our current level of knowledge) believes that the distant stars take time and space to transit. The inner workings of creativity state their close proximity to the life stream of Earth. The conscious acceptance of the unity within all allows for the distant stars to reach the plateau of awareness in an instant. What was distant now appears near. What does this have to do with the changes manifesting now? That which was distant is now near. The patterns of belief held by man came from a seeming distance of conscious and subconscious thought or patterns of the energy called conceptual beliefs. The changing life force is now nearer to the surface of conscious creation.

One change of man's belief is the distance of the stars made manifest in time and space. This distance is an illusion of concepts to participate in life as reality. The new now is to realize that the distance of your thoughts and ideals is not generated externally but internally as part of a group dynamic. This is a fact of reality as perceived by man not at the present time but in the near future.

Mother as Earth

The creation of Earth was dictated by the higher realms of thought. The evolution of Earth dictated that mankind develops into that which came forth from love. The fundamentals of life on Earth were to be a story of love. This can still take place if we awaken to the covenant that is the basis of our creation.

How Does This Event Impact Me?

Which way will you face when the sun rises? Will you face north, south, east, or west? Why is this important? The way you face indicates your current state of conscious awareness related to the life-giving rays of the sun. The level of consciousness you exhibit is related to your connection with life as you know it. The time of the rising sun is like an image of illumination on the landscape of the consciousness of one and all. The time to be aware is never given just as a gift. Time to be aware is an opportunity. Now is the time to realize that your existence is the inner and outer illumination of your ideals, your beliefs that manifest your creative life path. The dawning of a new perception is now.

What awakens one to the truth: an outer source or an inner spark? One awakens to the truth as a progression of spiritual expansion. One is truth. The divine right to truth is a given. The soul and its creations awaken when one becomes aware that truth exists. The road to truth is a journey, and that journey is a gift of the creative. The call to truth exists for each spark of divine creation when time and space relinquish their hold on life's journey. Each and every spark comes to a moment when it crosses the divide of opposites to unity. Listen, and the call is heard.

From the higher realms of existence, creativity is not seen as good or bad. It is seen as an expression of intent to create in material form and substance. Creativity is the constant of a lifetime. Creativity is your impression of self in a material form of expression.

It is the form of expression you choose for life that is being questioned. Why do I do what I do when I do it? Ask the question. Because life does not question its habits or beliefs. Habits and beliefs function in the world based on the symbols of life they accept as their path of creation. Man accepts that which is in the surrounding environment. Mankind accepts the illusion of life as a form of existence. The path appears to be based on availability. Availability is based on the perception of the world of opposites. For example, because water can be cold or hot, the composition of opposites is accepted. We accept what is the appearance of opposites as a way to exist in this realm. We choose our paths of existence based on the existing norms. Part of our challenge is to realize that there are alternatives that we do not experience because of our focus on the path we have accepted as ours. If an ingredient comes along to help you awaken, the process has an igniter or stimulation mechanism. This is the time when man's cosmic journey has encountered a process by which change in beliefs and accepted unstable reality can be addressed.

This is a time of transition. The focus is self, for that is where the game of life is created and accepted. That moment when you are created with the spark of life is a moment of joy for most. The moment of death is a moment of sadness for many. In between life and death, there is an option: create in the realm of conscious awareness or remain in a fog of total acceptance of fate. The difference is extreme when measured by the soul of creation. It is neither good nor bad. It simply is. It is the will of divine creation to make all things whole. How this is accomplished is up to the individual spark of creation that dwells within.

The form of one's life is not the subject of judgment; it is, however, the opportunity at this time to realize that options exist. Darkness does not only appear to shut out the light; it also conceals the availability of alternate possibilities. So too does a life-form that accepts the vibration of limited impressions of life. Awaken now in the realm of what is to determine the course of a new view of what will potentially be. I use the word *awaken* to present the reader with the cue to listen or receive a higher level of comprehension. If individuals are to do so, they must of their own volition move the needle of comprehension to a new awareness of life's possibilities.

Symbols of Life

I am not referring to the material symbols of life[5] as you know it but of the configuration of the design of mankind, which represents aspects of creation, which dictate manifest form. These are the symbols of life as they represent consciousness and in some circles: remembrance. When mankind sees the light of transition, there is a change in perception, as the symbols become real. Like many mandalas and symbols, such as the Star of David, the Holy Cross, the Flower of Life, the Tao and the image of the Sri Chakra, when one meditates on or contemplates the meaning or purpose, he or she is drawn into the consciousness that they represent.

Why Did You Choose a Labyrinth as a Symbol of the Emergence?

The name Tápu'at came to me as I slept early one morning. When I researched the name, I found that it meant "Mother Earth" or "mother and child," a labyrinth symbol from the Hopi nation. The meaning relates to the emergence according to Frank Waters in *Book of the Hopi*. As soon as I saw the symbol and its related

---

[5] The material symbols of life are what we use as our models for existence. Wealth has its symbols, as does power. Religion has its symbols, as does intolerance. Nations have their symbols, as do the political factions. The symbols of life are all around us, and for the most part, we accept them for what they are. How they register in our consciousness is an important part of being aware of how we are impacted by these symbols.

meaning, I knew intuitively it was related to the Cygnus event. I spent months trying to gain greater understanding of its meaning and the relationship it has with the Reveal Transit.

The labyrinth has come to mean seven aspects, or layers, of our experience in this time of transition. The aspects are like an unfoldment. The way into the labyrinth appears rather easy. The way out, however, requires a great deal of fortitude and desire to find the light of truth that is within and the world of truth that is our birthright. Refinement of self is like a labyrinth, not flat like you see on the pages of this book but multidimensional and filled with our doubts, fears, hopes, and dreams. Good and bad are not judged as opposites. It is what we do with life experiences and the gifts we are given that is the truth of our reality. The next few sections shed greater light on this statement.

Sun and Light

The sun and light now blend to create life with a different spectrum of creative capabilities. The potential embedded in light is unlimited by the laws of creation. The sun that brings the potential of existence is a blaze in the new form of creative expression—sun and light, light and sun. The blend is a force of nature that should be observed and revered not as a substitute for truth but as a vehicle to create with a greater understanding of the realities of life.

What Can I Do to Facilitate the Change Available to Us at This Time?

The clock of time in the realm of space is in fact the imagination of a greater form of reality. The way forward is a connection not as an *I* symbol but as a *we* or *us* consciousness. The old form of creative interpretation of life is based on group identification. This is the present level of life as it is recorded and interpreted. The true form of advancement is to realize unity, not as a cause but as a concept of wholeness. The way forward is available through the use of creative imagination. This is one step in the journey to a true form of reality.

The following is not the beginning of creative thought but the foundation for what is possible:

Align your thought with an intent to know the greater truth of your potential.

Sit with the light you perceive is real.

> Enter the heart through your intent to know the unity of conscious and unconscious realms.
>
> Listen to the heart, and focus your thoughts on one word: *life.*
>
> State simply, "Light is life."
>
> Allow the thoughts, images, and impressions to pass without judgment.
>
> Then state simply, "Light is love."
>
> Once more, allow the thoughts, images, and impressions to pass without judgment.
>
> Rest.
>
> Allow time and observation to lead you to a greater understanding of what light is in relation to life and love.
>
> This is the part of the journey; take time to enjoy the gift of presence.

Buddic Consciousness[6]

This entity is not a thought, icon, or being of worship but a stream of consciousness. It is above the mainstream of awareness. It is going beyond the limits of present-day awareness to reveal a greater truth. Mankind dwells in a sea of conscious-laden intent. What works for some works for all. The issues are awareness and desire, not as they currently appear as reality but as they are in light. Form and content are one in what is truth. There is a requirement that we awaken within ourselves to what is truth and its relationship to light's dynamics.

What Is the Next Aspect of Creation's Flow?

Time to dwell on the form of reality that binds mankind from the veil of oneness. The forms of matter and consciousness that we currently experience seem to separate us, not unify us. That which is appears not to attract but to repel. What is mankind to do in such an environment of creative thought? The answer lies in the direction of the moment, one in which mankind can realize a new dynamic of thought. That thought is oneness of ideals, and of a desire to bring about some form of unification.

The time to realize a greater truth is now. That truth is an indwelling desire to complete the journey we began long ago in terms of time and space. This journey of humanity is a lost idea in the stream of conscious thought and mainstream concepts. The travels of the Israelites from Egypt are a vague reminder of this journey, but it has been concealed in the mysteries of the ancient ways of verbal transmission. The journey of then is a journey of now.

---

[6] According to the *Llewellyn Encyclopedia*, the Buddic plane is the fourth plane up from the physical, sometimes called the intuitional level. I can only tell you that the obvious is sometimes right in front of us, and either we don't see it or we choose not to look for it.

The bondage of the Israelites symbolizes the bondage of our egos to a pattern of reality that is based on illusion. Moses symbolizes the emancipator, and the Red Sea symbolizes love. This is a brief explanation of why we are crossing the Red Sea to a reality that is based on light and not darkness. Concealed no more is the direction this journey can now take.

Through conscious intent, mankind can realign his thinking to the incoming consciousness of universal thought. Individuals can bring about a change not seen in prior cycles of related evolution. The one way to bring about this change from repulsive to magnetic attraction is through the faith in their ability to create as a unified force of equals. This means mankind is about to enter a world where the light of knowledge is combined with the light from within, making this an unparalleled leap in consciousness. The journey is not about how but about who will find that inner spark to make the opening of consciousness a priority for the advancement of the civilization of humanity. The time and place are here and now. Focus on a higher form of expression in alignment with inner peace. The way forward is the next breath in light.

Additional Thoughts on the Six Questions

The way forward is blessed by our desire to give truth its day in our lives. We are a collective of thoughts, ideas, and beliefs. We are individual in nature, as seen from form and conscious and subconscious content. We are one as a life-form, but we perceive only separation and distance. We believe we are created as flesh, and this adventure in life is guided by fate and destiny. We see limit and lack and understand the concept of pain and suffering, or so we think and most certainly believe. We are creatures of the land, but we have learned to fly. We see humanity as a mixed bag of color, race, religion, sex, and language. We are reason and extremes. The one constant is that Earth is our sustaining grace, and most of the time, we forget that vital ingredient in our journey through space and through the corridors of time.

Once, when man was created, there was an opportunity to find unity in creation. That opportunity was lost when man accepted the internal call to realize separation from the spark of his existence. We are not privy to the details and timing of this decision, but the consequences are apparent in the current moment.

Here is the moment when separation and limitation meet in the atmosphere of a world about to face a monumental challenge. This challenge is a result of the energies of constructive thought meeting the energies of destructive tendencies. As the saying goes, "Something has to give." We are in a stream of conscious and subconscious interaction that needs to welcome the emerging concepts of evolution that require us to realize we are going to alter our path of consciousness and journey through life.

The emergence from darkness is not meant to judge whether darkness is good or bad. The evolution of mankind can be seen from higher worlds as that of children learning their way around the environment they have been born into. They accept and mirror the models of their surroundings. They do not judge while they explore. It is when they are told and shown limits that they pull back from their exploration. They have a tendency to believe what they are told and accept, to one degree or another, through the rituals of their time. Time goes on, and there is progress in the way of life. Knowledge is acquired from universal sources and shared in a variety of ways. Some grow strong and excel, and others just seek to exist, but life goes on.

There are many themes played out at different levels. The desire for knowledge and exploration is either nurtured in childhood or left to the individual. Some appear to succeed, and others fail according to their state of conscious values, but the race of man moves seemingly forward. Darkness in this scenario is simply a lack of knowledge, insight, and understanding. It is a place of fear and restriction. Darkness appears as an absolute, when in reality, it is an option. It is a choice. Only the strong will survive? This is not true. What is true is that the options or choices we are presented with provide the direction of our journey individually and collectively. The realization that we have choices is not based on strength; it is based on knowledge. It is based on an understanding that the truth of our reality lies in a place of our essence. Without knowledge, there is darkness. Is it good or bad, or is it something to be aware of?

The way forward lies at the heart of the emergence of mankind from his seeming lack of knowledge to a realization that there is something else, something that in the midst of our wandering seeks recognition: one, we journey through the labyrinth of our creative adventure; two, we have reached a crossroads of sorts as we attempt to move forward; and three, the current level of our awareness seeks something else, something that is not limiting in its approach to life.

Imagine a path in which all things are possible. How do we get to that state of mind? How do we get beyond our current beliefs and our acceptance of what is? How do we realize that each of us is not an individual with a destiny but a life force that is not one but a conscious collective of wholeness?

The life force that is exceeds the limits of consciousness through attention to what is currently known by being aware, by seeking a greater knowledge. The wisdom of the time is to realize the inadequacies of the present moment and seek truth. The time of the present situation is one of opportunity. How does one push the energies of a lifetime to seek greater awareness? By being willing to learn and to take that knowledge to another level of understanding. Seek within for greater understanding of the link between man and the light from divine sources. Search present awareness for the role one plays in the unity of man and not division. Understand that thought is flexible when the intent is to gain a greater sense of self, not as an isolated entity but as part of the wholeness of life.

At the end of each section, there will be what I call wisdom stratums. These questions or statements are meant to be pondered. They are stepping-stones to a new level of thought and contemplation.

First Wisdom Stratum

What happens to freedom when it is not used?

    Can you define *freedom*?

Every man, woman, and child is free to use his or her gifts according to his or her direction in life. Do you know what gifts you have been given and how to use them?

Section 2

*

Some Things to Think About

The Path of the Labyrinth

How do you feel this day? How comfortable are you with life as you know it this day? The time to awaken from slumber is at hand. This is not a decree. It is a request. You are of importance to the universe. Do you know that? You are part of a mosaic of life, and you as a life-force have meaning. This is not made up to make you feel good or bad. It is a fact of third-dimensional reality and beyond. You are an ingredient in the flow of history, and for some reason, it has been kept a mystery. You and only you hold the key to the cause of your existence. What is the meaning of being? What is the key to your destination? As we travel through the labyrinth of third-dimensional reality, we should keep in mind that there are many paths but only one journey. The path you are on is the key to the great mystery of existence. One's purpose is a logical answer, and in part, that is true, but there is a greater mystery to your journey. That is the subject of this material.

You came into being as a soul wrapped in the material body we call physical. This body was created for a reason, as were you—the reason of reasons, the cause of creation. You are a life-form of immense capability, a soul wrapped in a vehicle that, in most cases but not all, possesses sight, sound, touch, taste, and smell. Swami Sri Yukteswar stated that these attributes are "five different energies that we have to learn to control." I suggest that these energies are gifts of creation so that you may learn to be an expression of your greater self. The knowledge of who you are was given to you long before birth and is embedded in the attributes you came into existence with. They are your tools of that knowledge. For some, this is easily understood, but for the majority of us, it is not. That is where the mystery lies. At the feet of mankind is a threshold that, once crossed, closes the door of memory and knowledge. Now is a good time to remember that you are here for a reason. Life is not a giveaway or happenstance. Life is the embodiment of something special. It is the comings and goings of creation, the levels of which are not the subject of this material.

Once, there was a sage sitting by the side of a mountain temple. A young visitor came upon the sage and asked if he knew which road the young man should take on his journey through life. The sage thought for a moment as the young man waited with great expectation. The sage finally spoke. "It is the road you are already on," said the wise man.

Each being gifted with life is already on his or her path. The question is this: Do you realize this truth? The next question is this: Do you know where you are going? Furthermore, do you know how to get there? For some, these questions have little to no importance, for either they just don't care, or their beliefs have created a path of finite intent and focus. If there is interest or a deeper desire to know more, read on, and if not, that is okay too, for you see, each path is a journey that accords with laws, not thoughts of or implemented by man. In plain English, all is as it should be when it comes to the path you are on. You live with the direction in life that you choose. It is not good or bad; it simply is.

The path of life is a journey to a destination of your choosing. The path, however, is the road of renewal. This is a dream, but within this dream, there are options. You can choose to participate to the fullness of your being, or you can choose a role based on present beliefs. Your choice can lead to a greater understanding of self and the gifts you possess or you can continue to accept what your present beliefs dictate. The choice is up to you. All have consequences. Action is a choice. Inaction is also a choice. The flow of this information is directed towards those who choose to understand and participate in the coming changes that are taking place in the world.

The path of awareness calls for an explanation from an inner source. Light is the evolution of man when he lifts up his eyes to see the connection between the stars and himself. The road of creation is one of unlimited possibilities. The infinite number of stars both seen and unseen gives just a hint of a higher order of existence, a future in which mankind realizes he is part of a greater whole, part of the community of life, which is as abundant as it is diverse. Today the same abundance and diversity exist on a plane where knowledge is kept in darkness, and light is misunderstood for the true nature of its radiance. Can you guess where this plane is?

How do we cope with the limits employed by mankind in his beliefs of separation and limitation? The answer is written in the wind. The answer is written in the winds of change. The answer is not only written; it is the message being given in this material and in other books that will be forthcoming. You see, the dynamics of change require layers to be peeled away so that beliefs are not only understood but also transmuted to a higher level of consciousness that leads to universal change. I realize the venture is full of challenges, but if the climb to the mountaintop were easy, when would we rejoice? We also must realize that this material is only part of a greater effort by others who have their pieces of the great mosaic of life.

The path of existence is like a labyrinth full of twists and turns, filled with the feeling that you are close to the true self, and then life moves on, and the road grows dim. All is as it should be. It is your conscious intent that gives rise to the challenges of your journey. If you say you intend to do something, do you truly mean it? Are you steadfast, patient, and clear in your direction? These are not idle verbs; they are action items. They require you to commit. There should be no vacillation on your part, only a clear step-by-step approach to the life you choose to live.

It is time for you to be open to a new point of view. This is based on you as a life force on the path of life. You are a gift of creation wrapped in the physical form of third-dimensional reality. Your awareness is limited to your gifts of existence and the way you have used those gifts to date. My role is to remind you that the mystery of who you are is not a deep, dark secret. On the contrary, everyone you meet shares your secret. We are all part of a network of souls that come together for a purpose. That purpose is not what you think or believe. It is the measure of a greater intention that draws us together. The light of your efforts is to get the highest use of your abilities from and with one another. This seems in conflict with the dysfunction and random destruction we see in the world, but it is true. The realm of creative opportunity seeks union of effort and expression. The beliefs of the time and the impact of cause and effect seem real. This is one of our greatest challenges. How do we come together to create unity when the present moment appears as it does?

Based on the following thoughts, judgment appears to be an obstacle to our achieving unity with one another. The other challenge is focused on fear.

Obstacles on the Road to Unity

Judgment drives many aspects of life. Judgment is like a qualifier of the life one leads. Judgment is the ability to assign a person to his or her proper place in the universe. Judgment is the resting place of justice. Judgment qualifies who we think we are. Judgment layers reality and lies like a blanket covering truth. Judgment is a game of making things up that are assigned to reality. Judgment is the superior or inferior nature of man's consciousness.

When people judge, they do so with a sense of authority, a sense of knowing. Judgment is not made without some corresponding action or event. Judgment is mainly based on belief. Belief, in this case, is as arbitrary as the wind. Direction of belief leads to judgment. What one judges to be true is based on societal norms. Though one is judged to be guilty on one side, one can be innocent on the other side, based on one's point of view.

No one is without judgment. No one walks this land without this gift. The question is the usage of judgment. How, when, and where is judgment used? Do you use judgment to satisfy your position, beliefs, or fears? Has judgment taken over and made you inflexible? What energy do you give to judgment of any kind? How kind and compassionate are you when judging? Do you see the person as guilty or innocent? Do you listen to your internal or external words as you place judgment on anyone or anything?

Left or right, as you move through life, you are given choices. On one hand, there is judgment, and on the other, there is discernment.

Webster's dictionary states that *discernment* is "the ability to judge well." The other definition is "perception in the absence of judgment with a view to obtaining spiritual direction and understanding." One definition of *judgment* is an opinion or conclusion. Judgment then is the use of energy to fix in your mind a direction of intent as relates to yourself or others. Discernment then is withholding energy to wait for insight of a higher nature. When one judges, he or she uses energy to facilitate that judgment. When one seeks greater clarity, one withholds judgment, which allows the use of energy to be focused on the path ahead.

Judgment by its very nature is a state of involvement that can serve as a distraction on your path and your journey through life. There is a quality to life that does not judge, for it sees the underlying perfection in all acts, big and small. This is not an easy subject to discuss outside of the ancient mystery schools. The use of discernment is the use of a facility you were given before birth. It is the beginning of a capability that allows you to conserve your energy force. This force is then available to allow for greater reception of your internal guidance. Judgment is like a TV program that takes your attention and occupies your consciousness as someone in the other room is talking to you. This form of distraction takes your focus away from the journey you have before you.

The path of life is filled with many opportunities. How many are missed because you are distracted by other things, such as judgment? The other day, I was looking for a bottle of flaxseed oil. I knew it was on the second shelf of a cabinet. I reached up to take it out of the cabinet, and the bottle wasn't there. I thought, *Well, my wife must have moved it.* I looked on the first shelf—no bottle. I then went to get the small stepladder to look on the third shelf. *Why would my wife put it on the third shelf?* The bottle was not on the third shelf either. This was nuts. I knew the bottle was on one of the shelves. My wife said, "Let me look." She has a knack for finding things I don't. She walked up to the ladder and points to the counter. "What's that?" she asked. It was the bottle of flaxseed oil I was searching for. It was right at my belt buckle. The amount of energy in the stories I made up in my head had been a total waste. I'd judged who moved the bottle, the motive for moving the bottle, and its location. None of it was right. I know a lesson and a waste of energy when I experience it.

Judgment is not fixed, but it is if you continue to judge people and situations in the same way. Judging someone is an opportunity if you choose to view it that way. If the desire is there, you can catch yourself in the act of judging. You can ask yourself why you're judging someone or some situation. Why do you think something is right or wrong? Could there possibly be another explanation to a story or event? If you interrupt the process of judging, you have a chance to review how you are using energy to distract yourself from the course of your journey.

In the ancient mystery schools, there was a doorway that stated "To thine own self be true." The use of judgment is, in most cases, not used for a higher purpose. The way of the now is to realize that as a creative expression of the divine, you have the ability to focus your energy in such a way that you gain greater clarity as you venture along life's pathway. Judgment distracts from the true self that resides within.

The eye of mankind, based on our beliefs and accepted reality, comes to the conclusion that all is separate. Our minds are conditioned to perceive differences and judge the world we see and believe is real. That which appears is a form of consciousness that accepts the limits and limitations of now and the future. Those become the limits of perception and thought. The mind knows what the mind knows based on what? Reality is the stage of expression within the limits of accepted beliefs. If you believe your religion is better than another, the judgment of inferior versus superior takes place. If you believe your car is better than your next-door neighbor's, the judgment of inferior versus superior is present. If you ask your heart with a sincere desire to know truth, you will find that superior-versus-inferior judgment does not appear. Why is that so?

Let us view judgment for a moment. To judge is to determine if one finds a separate state of action, belief, or knowing acceptable or lacking. One bases judgment on the screen of accepted beliefs, thoughts, and ideals. Judgment is a state of mind based on the fear that one is incomplete. This fear is embedded in the atmosphere of preconceived ideals. Where is judgment's realm? Take the vibration of unconditional love, and you will see, feel, or experience calm and a sense of expansion. It appears as a rolling motion of repeated cycles. Take the vibration of judgment, and watch, feel, or experience the limited peaks and valleys of the act. One is harmonious in form, and the other is sharp and without clear definition. Judgment is a defense against the norms of accepted beliefs of self or group consciousness. This defense is an absolute way of protecting one's self-identification. One judges what one perceives as an act outside of projected self-imposed behaviors. This can happen individually, in groups, in nations, or on a worldwide basis. Most judgment is destructive. We know that some judgment appears to protect or give comfort or compassion to others. We see a need and supply a helping hand. When did judgment transform itself from harm to help? There are two aspects of judgment here: one of separation and one of unity.

The first aspect is to become a judge—to determine fault and draw a conclusion, to take sides and invoke who is right and who is wrong. The details appear to be clear, and one has taken a side. The process of duality functions but not at a level that is easily understood. The energy of duality is not one of balance; duality is an extreme when seen from the use of energy. The line of thinking is to create a state of nonjudgment, which allows for the judge to be judgeless. It's a state of mind not easily accomplished based on the dualistic thoughts we maintain.

The second aspect is to see a need. How you judge someone's misfortune comes from the heart, not the mind. That enables you to move easily from witness to participant. When one judges someone in need from the mind, there is sympathy maybe, but there is little to no action. When the heart identifies the level of misfortune, the instinct to act is immediate. The mind separates, and the heart combines. This is a subject to ponder.

The current events of 2017 have shown us our ability to come together when we see or feel an urge to act. The level of compassion that we feel drives us to act in selfless ways. What is it within us that overrides our normal response to life and motivates us to bring forth the love that is within us? Could it be that for one moment in time our normal beliefs are dropped to demonstrate a greater truth that exists within us?

Cygnus Light

The Challenge of Fear

Fear is the great divider. Fear is the home of isolation. Fear is the motivating factor of darkness in thought and belief. How does fear work? It starts with a belief that at some point, you will not be safe. At some point, there will be an event that seems to be beyond your control. Fear is an expression of pain. Fear is the belief that darkness holds a menacing force. Fear is the acceptance that the unknown holds danger. Fear is a source of weakness on one hand, and on the other, it's an excuse to strike out at others in self-defense. Fear is the extreme option as a form of expression. Fear is the identity of the ego. Fear is the acceptance that God, our Source, is somewhere else. Fear diminishes and is a form of expression that is a source of discord.

Why do I focus on fear at this juncture? The way forward seeks balance. The way forward is an ideal. How can you move forward in life when you have something holding you back? How can you make steady progress when the balance of your steps is unsure and uneven? Balance, in this scenario, is the measure of creating what is to be with a sense of purpose and clear intent. How can you move through life with clarity when you are unsure of your steps? The line of creation is not straight. The steps or processes of creation follow a path that accords with nature and its laws. The way forward through the path of the labyrinth is the way of completion. You, the traveler, and the path of destiny are one and the same. The steps of your journey are being designed by you based on your thoughts, beliefs, life expectations, and life lessons. You might think this is overwhelming. "I have no idea what my life lessons are," you might say. If you pay close attention to the life you have led and are leading, you may glean a sense of what your lessons are. With sincere effort, you can identify many of your beliefs and what you expect from life. However, it may seem beyond one's ability to grasp all that has been described. Some may see this as a challenge and begin to delve deeper into their beliefs. Some may seek the help of professional life coaches or practitioners they feel may help open doors that have been closed for some time. Others may believe this is the way they are, and that's fine. Others may think this reality is beyond their knowledge and capabilities and continue along life's path.

Let's go back to fear for a moment. The challenge is to realize that all of the work required to accomplish your goal in life is within you. Fear of the unknown is present, as is the fear of finding out something about yourself that is not good based on your value system or your internal self-assessment. First, we are required to face fear directly. Realizing you are fearful of something requires awareness and a willingness to acknowledge that fear exists. Second, it takes courage to seek a meeting, if you will, with whatever fear you have identified. Third, it takes a willingness to let go of your fear. The possibility of losing a fear may be uncomfortable. Let me tell you why.

Fears can become like companions. They become so ingrained in the psyche that they become the embodiment of what is feared. The limits that are created are not just restrictive. They lead to all forms of experiences that justify the fears. Like attracts like. Fear has another attribute. It attracts people of like mind, thus fortifying the life experience. Fear is false when one realizes the fear started from an event, something modeled in the formative years, a thought that was deep-seated, involvement with an event that happened to someone else, or a belief in a future event or happening. Fear can also be based on judgment, and that is where guilt comes in. Fear is the application of a concept based on a lack of understanding of life experiences. The face of fear is like a solid event. It is fixed and strong when belief is allowed to be free of the foundation of love. As addictive as fear is, it is transitory when faced directly. Its impact can be significant, but the end result can be uplifting when fear is replaced with the light of understanding. Now we speak of fear as an obstacle, but the will within man can overcome obstacles when used within the framework of knowledge.

Today is a good day to banish fear. Every day is a good day to be without fear, to be fearless. Fearlessness is a goal worth achieving, because it allows you the opportunity to walk the path on your journey of life with the attitude that nothing is impossible. There is a saying: "Expect a miracle." That indicates that nothing is impossible. Nothing is outside the realm of possibilities. In the Infinite Mind of Creation, all things are possible. Let us start with the thought, the ideal, that all things are possible. Fear does not see that as a key to experience. If all things are possible and I maintain a fearless attitude, it will be impossible for me to manifest my fears. The issue is realizing that you can and will manifest fears in one form or another. "If I can manifest fear, why can't I eliminate fear?" you might ask. You can with the right frame of mind, direction, and knowledge.

What do I mean by the right frame of mind? I mean the direction of thought that reflects a willingness to observe when fear is generated. Notice how it is triggered and what you do with it when it enters your life stream. The right frame of mind at the beginning of rising above fear is awareness. How you use your ability to observe your action and reaction to the stimulus of fear is just the beginning of the process.

The right direction is based on your intent. What is your intent when something fearful takes place? Many times, we react to fearful situations without thinking. Our reaction seems to be automatic, something beyond our control. The other day, my wife and I were walking along a dam near our home. As we started up an incline, a big black bee came at my wife. It must have been two inches long and, with its wingspan, at least three to four inches wide. We had never seen a bee that big before. My wife tried to push it away, and it came at me. I took my cap off and swung at it. To my amazement, it came right back at me. I swung again, and it came at me again. As I went to swing one more time, I took a step back and lost my balance. Thankfully, my head just missed a metal railing, but I hit my back and elbow. When I got up, the bee was nowhere to be seen. Both of us had hit our fear buttons big-time. We have been walking and hiking for years and never encountered anything like that. Because I was writing this material, I realized that was an event I had to learn from.

We were under attack, and my first, second, and third reactions were to strike out. I did not want to kill the bee, but I wanted to send it on its way. I have seen carpenter bees in the past that were big but not that big. I realized that my reaction to the perceived attack was to strike out, and by doing so, I lost my balance with painful results. A bleeding elbow and bruised back were the results of my reaction to what took place. *How can I learn from this event?* I asked myself. *And what will I do differently if something like that happens again?* What I didn't know at the time was that we were to have two more encounters with carpenter bees. The result of the first encounter was that I am now more aware of my reaction when a bee, wasp, or carpenter bee comes buzzing around. I determined not to repeat my actions and reactions. Learning to find balance and maintain a composed response in a fearful situation like that was a good lesson for me.

Since that time, my wife and I have had two other encounters with carpenter bees. The first two times they seem to go after my wife first, and as I try to chase them away, they go after me. The second time it happened, we were walking along a hiking trail in the mountains near our home. The bee once more went after my wife and I swung my cap to chase it away. The bee then came directly at me. I calmly stood my ground, made sure I was in a balance stance, and hit it squarely with my cap. I was happy to see it fly away uninjured. I felt a sense of relief that I had learned a lesson from our first experience. It was a lot less painful. The third time was amazing. I was on my back patio, looking out at the clouds, and I suddenly realized a carpenter bee was flying right at me. Without thinking, I let the bee come directly at my face, and without any fear, I took a deep breath and blew on it. It must not have liked my breath, because it flew away.

Knowledge versus fear—that is the beginning of a journey worth taking. The information you are about to receive is from the wisdom of ancient mariners on the sea of life.

What is knowledge? Knowledge is the information necessary to complete a task for which you are qualified. Knowledge is education and experience. Knowledge is also the awareness required to expand your capabilities. It is information that allows you the ability to make informed decisions and actions consistent with that information's insight.

Fear is an obstacle of the journey you are on. Fear is an illusion based on the notion that you are within the physical body and must be protected. Fear is the receiver of energy that is not qualified as an expression of the Infinite Mind.

Love appears to many as the opposite of fear. To me, love has no opposite. Love gives; it does not hold back. Love is the perfect expression of creation when nothing is expected in return. Love is not an isolator; it is a unifier. Love gives, expecting the best. When one is fearful, he or she expects the worst. I guess many would say, "You have just reinforced that love is the opposite of fear." The fine point of duality is to get caught in a game of back and forth. To be fearless is a state of being.

Why do I bring up love at this point? To show you that there is an opposing form of action you can take. Fear appears to dominate. That role was given by man, not our Creator. The defining element of fear is that it has no basis; in fact, it has no mooring to hold on to when love is present. The light of understanding is getting brighter now.

After receiving the above information, I asked for a way to banish fear.

Here is the answer:

Locate fear through self-awareness.

Do not prepare for combat.

There is nothing to fear.

The energy of fear is belief. Withhold belief.

Realize fear for what it is: transparent and fluid.

Turn to a higher form of thought: trust and gratitude.

Release fear by allowing it to move outside of your awareness.

Do not bid fear adieu.

See a new horizon with the sun growing brighter.

Say to yourself, "Nothing was with me but a dream that has gone into the rising sun."

See a road before you that is clear and ready for you to travel on.

Your belief created fear. Your belief in your capacity to create anew gives you direction.

The Fear Factor

The focus on fear as a challenge to our growth continued.

That which is faced with the light of knowing is not based on fear but on the premise of oneness. Fear is more than a four-letter word. Fear is an emotion, and it is an anticipation of a disruptive event. Fear is a lesser vibration that appears magnified as a life-altering event. Fear is a reinforcement of a belief in a disconnect from love. Fear confirms isolation and reinforces the belief in pain and suffering. Fear's opposite is a calm certainty of events. It can be seen as a way to perpetuate habits and beliefs in life. Fear is a disruptor of commonplace things and events. Fear's isolation supports the notion that all of life is disengaged from oneness. Hope is replaced by uncertainty, and uncertainty provides the field where fear dwells. Fear is not the opposite of love, for love has no opposite when seen from a plane of knowledge and wisdom.

All of mankind experiences fear to one degree or another due to several factors, including the lack of awareness of the creative capacity of life; the unknown aspect of life when one lives moment to moment without faith; the complete and total belief in suffering; the lack of knowledge of unity, of oneness, which gives one pause to venture into unchartered territory; the ego as a form of presence based on protection of self-identity; and the way of fear as a road through darkness that believes in possessions as something of value. This could be anything material, mental, or emotional.

Fear is a factor in creation's realm as an identifier of things to be lost, not gained. The realm of fear is real because of the value placed on whatever can be lost or taken away. Fear is a possibility, not necessarily an actuality. Fear is the door of opportunity when faced for what it represents. Fear cries for identification, not for perpetuation but for completion. Fear is not a pit of negativity; it is a lesson to be overcome. We must rise above it with a purpose and a sense of peace. Fear is our identification with other. It is defensive, and it is offensive. In either case, it is not based in love. It is an extreme that is out of balance with one's ability to create in light. Fear appears real and will materialize with repetition and energy.

Fear's magnetic pull is based on the stuff of beliefs. It is wrong thinking, as it creates boundaries. The lack of something is not fear-based; it is the result of an ingrained concept of life that does not understand potential.

What is potential? It is the one aspect of creation that has no limits, no boundaries, and no illusions. It is the open state of creation. Fear is its limiting factor. Fear perceives potential as something less than the infinite creation of life.

Fear is an acceptance of current states of existence and is not in balance with one's life path. Fear could be ancient in origin, part of present life experiences, or something to resolve through right action. Fear could also ask for correct thinking from the mind or the heart. For some reason, I thought back to an event that took place with Mildred Norman, who became known as the Peace Pilgrim. She walked more than twenty-five thousand miles across the United States with a message of peace. She was physically assaulted on one of her walks, and her response was to come from her heart, not from fear. Her attacker soon ran out of whatever it was that had caused him to attack her. If this was a test, Peace Pilgrim obviously passed it. She became the embodiment of what she shared with so many, a living symbol of what peace is: an expression of love.

This material does not condone physical violence of any kind, whether it be to right a wrong or as a victim. Physical violence is the result of fear in action. It is the result of accepted conduct in life as a way to express oneself. It is false identification with the gifts of life.

Fear's undoing is based on awareness. It is the result of seeking harmony. Eliminating fear is an internal longing for a higher form of expression. Fear's demise is based on a realization that worlds were not created through fear; they were created through a desire to grow and evolve. The knowledge and wisdom embedded in life seeks to move forward with an unrestricted flow. How can this be achieved with the current state of consciousness being what it is?

We must realize that life has a purpose, and that purpose is to seek harmony. The patterns of reality seek a harmonic expression that is consistent with the laws of nature and indwelling capabilities of mankind. They seek a reversal of present-day thinking and a willingness to learn what is inherent in their ability to create and to learn and accept the responsibility that life is for all and not a select few. Each and every breath is a gift, and it is important to realize what that truly means.

Some things to consider:

> Awareness: Become aware of the thoughts that give rise to fear. Do not wrestle mentally with your fearful thoughts; just observe.

> Detachment: Gently, in a state of awareness, allow your thoughts and emotions to play out, hopefully while nothing is materializing.

> Identification: After a fearful thought or emotion has passed, seek within your state of awareness to locate the source of the fear. Do not try to steer the answer. Allow it to identify itself. This may take some practice.

> Soul: If you are able to identify the source of the fear, gently ask your soul to hear your request to release the source of your fear. Say, "I am worthy to

be free of all negativity, and I release the cause and
substance of this imbalance. Here and now, I accept
my worthiness as a road to greater clarity on my life
path. I am worthy. Yes, I am."

Release is just a word with no value, without intent. Let us
now go over the two aspects related to fear that are vital for relief,
clearing, and balance. The first is release. We are the opening of a
door to the inner workings of the mind and heart. Here we struggle
with understanding how fear is a factor in our existence. It is not
without cause when the world around us demonstrates a lack of
understanding of love and respect. It is the opposite of unity that
is on display throughout one's life cycle. Fear is the companion of
separation, and separation is a major issue in this world. It leads to
false identification and imbalances of causes and effects without
end, or so it seems.

The word *release* signifies "letting go." How simple that sounds
until you go to release anything you have given value to. That
may seem strange, but it is true. We all have, to some extent, given
our fears a value. If they had no value, why would we keep them?
It makes sense to hold on to something of value, but why, of all
things, fear? The timeline is based on the mixture of events, beliefs,
and life lessons you accept as real. You see, if you did not believe,
either consciously or subconsciously, that what gave rise to fear is
real, you would not have assigned that fear the space it occupies in
your reality. Fear is not just a four-letter word. It is an opportunity
to realize the limits fear has placed on the world and its inhabitants.

The ego has been given as a cause of fear, but that is just a name,
a label. The fear of man is not just one big ego. The separation from
the Source that we accept as real is certainly a contributing factor
to our belief in fear.

Mankind has dwelled in the Garden of Eden and eaten the
forbidden fruit that brought to light his seeming separation from
the Tree of Life. When one dwells in a state of separation, he or she

senses that something is missing. That something is in the form of one's birthright. What was given that is no longer there? The truth of existence is and will be mankind's goal for as long as the separation from the Source is accepted as anything other than a dream. The ego and Source are not the issue. The issue appears to be that we are not consciously aware that there is a missing ingredient to our flow of consciousness and to the fullness of our birthright.

Now mankind crosses a divide of sorts. The way forward is through the realization that fear is a product of evolution. It is a device that imposes limits and, on an internal level, restricts conscious and unconscious thoughts. Fear is a restrictor of potential at the point of origin. Now, at the crossroads of conscious evolution, fear is faced as an opportunity. When fear is realized for what it is, there is an opening in consciousness. However slight that opening may be, it gives one an opportunity to release fear's attraction. The release of fear is the release of self from a bondage of self-imposed restriction. The world at large will not cooperate with the release of fear on a universal scale.

What does that mean for you as an individual? The way to release fear is folded like a lotus flower before it blooms. The ingredients are there; it just waits for the call of its true impulse to reveal itself. What are the ingredients I refer to?

> First and foremost, it is imperative that one recognizes fear. Just the awareness is the signal for some form of conscious action to take place.

> Second, notice what response you or others have to the fear taking place. How is this altering the dynamics of your mind, heart, and feelings? Have you withdrawn from action, or have you taken action that is detrimental to yourself and others in some way?

Third, if you have been aware enough to observe the first two petals of the lotus, what is the current result of your fear? Are you upset? Do you sense that you have been physically altered in some way? Do you feel energized and uplifted by the events, or are you depressed, saddened, or disgusted with yourself and others? What is your mental and emotional condition at this time?

Fourth, do you currently accept your condition as normal? Have you processed this fear so often that you are conditioned to your response?

Fifth, how do you address these fears once you realize all of the above? Do you pray? Do you judge yourself for allowing this fear in your life? Do you take positive or negative action? If so, what?

Sixth, light in a dark room allows us to see our surroundings. We do not have to stumble blindly through the room or have wild imaginings of what is or isn't taking place. It is time to realize all fear for what it is. It weighs down the true nature of man. Fear's release is awareness made to perform the task of truth. Exactly what does that mean?

The answer is in the moment of recognition. It is the release of an energy that is not in harmony with creation. Fear is distance. Fear is not ease; it is dis-ease. Fear completes nothing of true value. Its growth is like a weed in a garden of flowers. Energy that binds is not energy of love, which frees. The way to release fear is through knowledge, awareness, and courage. Without courage, fear is a winner of the current status of life. One will go to heaven to find relief, but that is not the way of now. The way of now is a realization that you are sacred.

Beliefs

The light of a million stars shines now within the framework of mankind's realm of consciousness—the bright light of understanding of that which is hidden: the belief in a false form of identity. The darkness of eons has hidden, by the very nature of darkness, an image of true relationships with various forms of life. The light now present reveals a greater dimension of understanding of the forces of creative expression. What is belief? It is the connection of concepts that originated in the beginning and became accepted as fact. A belief is a thought that becomes so real that life seems to exist according to the guidelines of the belief. There are several levels of belief: individual belief, group or family belief, and mass belief. The latter starts with a concept or framework and transitions through time to allow for expansion and growth. The origins of the initial concept are not known to this author. The cause that created the initial effect is written in our hearts. We are products of the original cause. This does not imply sin. I am not currently conscious of that original cause.

Belief holds or binds us to a framework of avenues that limit our ability to see the entire picture of our reality. It makes vision narrow and confines us to our preconceived notions of reality. Our beliefs in third-dimensional creations are limiting us in many ways. To begin with, the journey of one is not seen as a journey of all. The focus of one eliminates the concepts of enlightened states of being for all based on self-judgment and self-identification.

Belief is the object of our daily existence. When we realize how limiting our current beliefs are, we are poised to move on to more productive adventures. The issue is that we are stuck with the current calendar of events, and we are a product of our beliefs. We hold on to these beliefs because they identify who we are. We see ourselves in one another based on our beliefs. Beliefs are security against nature and others. We have identified with our current life stream for so long that we have overlooked something of great importance: Truth.

Truth

When did belief become truth? Your truth is based on several factors, including birth, life models, spiritual or religious beliefs, and the experience of this and other lifetimes. Your truth is a product of your focus in the earthly realm. How do we reconcile these truths with one another? We seek out others who agree with our truth. We congregate at a level of nations, continents, languages, and ideologies to support our truths. No man is an island. Have you ever heard that statement? The denial or acceptance of that statement depends on your truth and your level of awareness.

Truth is not limited to one's perception of life and ideals. Truth is an underlying cause for existence. Truth is a spectrum of reality. When one focuses on truth, he or she realizes that one truth leads to another. In a sense, truth is the bearer of opposites.

Truth is the bearer of opposites. How can truth be the bearer of opposites? The way truth works is that it is an underlay or foundation of reality. What reality are we speaking of? This reality that is third dimensional in origin for starters.

Truth in the third dimension is made up of two main parts: the truth of what is currently termed *heaven* and the realm of duality and beliefs, the truth of Earth. Creation spoke to mankind and asked, "Do you see the light?" Mankind responded by saying, "I see the light of the sun and stars." Creation once more asked if mankind saw the light. Once more, mankind answered based on what he saw outside of himself. This response became man's truth. The mystery schools of the past and present offer a different response, one that is seen not outside the self but within. Which truth resides in the consciousness of man? That which resides in the mainstream of consciousness. Light is creation's vehicle of the dynamic of existence. What is the form of truth that resides as a conscious structure of existence?

The form is the content of the hierarchy of beliefs, meaning truth is seen in many layers. How do you identify the truth of existence? Not by being lucky, fortunate, or placed in a position of elevated thinking. The truth of existence is a gift based not on merit but on the strength of your dedication to what truth is, meaning the appearance of opposites is a lesson to learn as you journey to the truth of who you are.

In the realm of opposites, we can identify two truths: one that is the truth that you accept as you and all you survey; the second is the truth that is the foundation of existence. The greater truth is one that adheres to the laws of creation and not the laws of man. The first truth is a part of our consciousness that allows us the ability to express in a way that conforms to mankind's belief in reality. The second truth is concealed in the veils that limit our true nature to come forth. Searching for our greater truth is part of our journey through the labyrinth of life.

The Emergence

How refined is the finest element you can think of? How refined is the element of your conscious thought and ideals? The beginning of a new adventure is usually the end of a prior adventure. When one aspect of life ends, another usually takes its place. Continuity in life is rarely realized for what it is. The moment something, some event, or some relationship falls away, the continuity in life is felt as an uneven tremor or sharp jolt. When the same moment is seen or experienced through a different set of eyes, there is a realization that life continues, sometimes with a sense of sadness and loss or joy and expansion. The time of transition will have its ups and downs, or so it will seem, but life will continue.

The refinement of observation is required as the emergence of a new sense of living is experienced. The focus of today is to realize that there is a stream of consciousness that mankind is a part of. The continuity of life will bring forth many opportunities to realize that something is about to happen or is happening. The darkness of the approach to the days and nights that is currently being experienced will be challenged. New concepts of creation will spring up. It is important to discern which concepts come from fear and dominance and which come from knowledge and love. Because each life is part of the path of creation, it will be up to each person to decide where to place his or her faith.

It is important to remember that each life is a gift and a resource, not a hindrance, as you come into the awareness that this journey is part of creation. The call of your name is a powerful tool in the process of emergence. The right of one's will is the birth cry. The will provides you with many gifts. The Creator is one with the will in each and every soul. The use of will should never be given to another or to a group. This is a form of abdication of your birthright. It is ignorant to think our Creator would provide us with a gift we do not realize is of great importance. It is your vehicle of expression. When used to the fullest, it is the basis for love. When used periodically to create less than your potential, it is like a magnificent garden you have allowed to wither and die. When we do not use our will and we allow others to dictate our lives, we have allowed the gift we are to cease functioning. This lack of use of will is part of the age of darkness and has contributed in the past to a decline in the evolution of man.

The focus of the labyrinth is to allow us to realize that our path is ours to create. It is our responsibility to realize the greater truths we have been given in life to express. The form and content of our lives are who we are, and we are the path both individually and collectively. The journey through the labyrinth has great meaning because we are part of a great mosaic. Each life within the mosaic is precious, important, and worthy of every blessing the light of creation can bestow. We are not taught that we are precious, because the truth of our entry into life seems to be forgotten. How different would the world be if we all realized the precious gift we are?

The importance of your life is not based on ego values and machinations. It is based on your expression of the gifts you possess. This importance is not measured by status; it is the result of your growth as a human being and as a light in the firmament of the divine. This is not a throwaway statement. It is meant to convey an important message. We can judge who we think we are based on our value system, but the truth is, your heart and soul have a better grasp of where you stand on the path of evolution.

The Doorway of the Infinite
Mind of Creation

Beyond this doorway is a prize. Can you guess what it is? The prize is light. It's not the light you think of that lights your home or car headlights. No, this light is active, and it is energetic. It has within it the core of infinite possibilities and infinite knowledge. The light can be seen as divine, and it can also be seen as overwhelming. The light I speak of shines forth brighter than the brightest sun, but it is beyond the spectrum of human sight. No one owns this light, and it cannot be possessed. It flows from a great source that is indistinguishable. This light has an awareness not of individual pieces but of the totality of the whole. It knows nothing, but it knows everything. We are part of this light, but for some crazy reason, it eludes our consciousness and awareness.

The question at hand is this: What does this light represent, and if it is for our higher good, how do we access it? We must go back in time and space before we can go forward.

The reason for creation is lost in time. The patterns of reality that ripple across the universe now were in absolute stillness. The un-manifested was at rest. The seas of creation were in infinite slumber. Nothing was upon the face of this silent void. The creation of the process of creation did not exist as we understand existence. There was in this stillness a tremor, a movement that suddenly burst forth. The greatest of light filled the stillness, and there was movement. From the movement came another tremor from this newly created universe, and thought came forth. From this universe of universes, the thought became word, and the word traveled in the form we call dimensions. As dimensions upon dimensions manifested, there came a force. This force roared through the universes and through dimensions. In each was a receptivity, and the roar became something I will call vibration. Within these multitudes of sound, there was a further breakdown that became frequency and octaves. The intelligence of the original tremor seated itself within all there was. It became the totality of All There Is, Was and Will Ever Be. Life was created as a form of existence and took its place within the ALL. Cycles, rhythms, and forms of expressions began to manifest. Within the ALL, there was mind, and the mind proceeded to multiply and diversify. Expression became endless. The focus of life began as a tremor. The result of life will be to return to the great oneness from which we all came.

As a side note, I tried to comprehend in some small way what I was receiving. The words to describe this seem inadequate, as my inner sense felt I was being given a kindergarten version of what took place. If I have misstated anything I received, it is due to my inability to convey the information properly. The one thing I do realize is that the universe we reside in is alive and intelligent. Each life-form is just one expression of the word that traveled through all there is. We are part of a supreme galactic whole that includes other universes and dimensions. The number appears infinite. We are part of a living collection of life that is exquisite. Words cannot properly describe the totality of all there is. The infinite mind of creation is there for us to become aware of and learn from. It is the opening into the realm of possibilities that can take us to a new level of existence.

Since I wrote this last paragraph another insight has come to me. We are the projection of an idea. An idea that has its origin in a spectrum of life that is beyond words to describe. We came from this idea as a form of expression. Our expression is the result of this overriding idea. We are part of a creative intent that we seem to have forgotten. Each of us are part of this idea and this idea is something that I can only describe as sacred. The totality of what I am trying to describe is without any form, it is pure unrestricted knowledge.

The State of Man

What is the state of man and his kind? The fostering of beliefs in the dual roles of mankind, including good versus bad, light versus dark, and compassion versus hate, is a game of opposites. It is a reflection of the fragmentation of consciousness. By working in the realm of opposites, one must, when playing the game, choose a side. To sit on the sidelines and not choose is to be considered not a team player, one who is outside of society. The choosing of one side over another sets up competition and energy in opposition to whatever side you choose. This energy imbalance is the game of distraction. If you are on one side, then you are obviously not on the other. Your energy, thoughts, and beliefs are focused on winning, because you are right, and someone else most assuredly must be wrong.

How victorious is the world when the ones on the right-side win? How stable is the world when there is a winner and a loser? How prosperous is the world when everyone shares in the spoils of war, conflict, or opposing concepts of reality? Right versus wrong is a balancing game in which the winners never fully succeed because of the imbalances created by conflict. The truth is that light is not the bearer of right or wrong. Light is the bearer of the knowledge of truth. The light of the concept based in duality is not harmonious with the nature indwelling within.

Forget for a moment that you have the ability to choose. What you see as the movement of people is simply the movement of people. There is no left or right and no forward or away from you. There is just movement. The people are neither friendly nor unfriendly. You are not concerned with their looks, because you are not able to choose. What does that feel like? Can you even imagine what that feels like? Why do I ask such a ridiculous thing? I believe you have the ability to suspend judgment. You can isolate choice in such a way that the only gift becomes discernment. You can make a choice based on a higher wisdom. When we release the focus of our world on opposites, we rely on nonjudgment to guide our lives. In that lies the proper use of energy to reclaim a part of you that is distracted by the game of opposites.

The truth of the current moment is that all of mankind is one collective intelligence. This truth has been obscured from the mind of man. All of mankind functions in the realm of third-dimensional thought. The beliefs of the spectrum of creation based in third-dimensional thought are somewhat limited when the only thing you rely on is the human base of knowledge. The greater wisdom does not hold separation and opposites as prime values of existence. The greater wisdom sees the commonality of human spirit. The focus of one's lifetime can be on the survival of the entity. The greater wisdom focuses on the growth of the intellect as a member of the spiritual essence that is without boundaries. The greater wisdom is the focus of light on the planet and its growth in the universal plan of creation.

The time for the use of consciousness as a tool to glorify the self is coming to an end. The state of man is in flux. The change is not the idea of mankind but the influence of a great resource of power. This power source is the light of conscious correction. The light of illumination reveals a great truth. Mankind is capable of elevating his consciousness to a realm that is consistent with the laws of divine knowledge and expression, a realm where life is lived to fulfill the promise of creation and where the focus is not on survival but on the completion of one's role as an instrument of the divine. One's choice of roles is an opportunity to create not as it is presently seen by many, who wish just to get by, but to lift oneself past present norms to an elevated form of consciousness.

The right to life is a gift. The ability to love is likewise a gift. How many gifts has mankind received that have gone unopened? How many days, years, decades, and eons have gone by without the awareness needed to open the gifts? Sweet are the dreamers who have chosen the path of light. Sweet are the efforts of those on the way who have created better lives for themselves and others. Here is the first of many thoughts to open the heart and let in the gifts of creation. When God in heaven wrote that life is for the living, he was stating sacred knowledge. Life is divine because it is a gift. Life is sacred because it comes from the Source. Life is a divine gift from the Source.

Time is not conveniently here to provide us with the opportunity to age. Time is here to provide us with a sense of difference. How we use time is a matter of free will. The sages say that time is an illusion. I agree, but for most of us, time is a vehicle we can use if we are so inclined. Time is also a register of the state of human consciousness in relation to the cosmic community of which we are a part. In the previous sentence, I mentioned using time as a vehicle. To clarify, the vehicle I am referring to is your consciousness. The body you occupy experiences continual change, but one's consciousness can seem to reside in the past, present, and sometimes in daydreams or visions in the future. Because of our tendency to do things habitually, it appears our consciousness remains the same. This is not true; as we experience life, we learn on a continual basis. For many of us this process goes unnoticed or is lost in our preoccupation with the realm we dwell in. The question is this: What do we do with the knowledge? The answer to the experiences of life is our growth as individuals and as a society. The problem we have is that sometimes growth comes in the form of loss, destruction, and hatred. How can that be described as growth? The use of duality or opposites appears convoluted, but is it? The finer qualities of life call for balance. Sometimes the balancing of prior experiences requires what appear to be extreme, out-of-place reactions. Based on the current cycles, the totality of life is on an upswing. This means we can bring balance to our lives with kindness, compassion, and the thoughtfulness brought about by a sincere desire to go through life in harmony with our world and all it encompasses. Easily said but not easily accomplished.

The use of defined methods to achieve a greater sense of harmony is all around us. We just have to open ourselves to the greater truths that dwell within. Peaceful means are at hand when we choose our actions based on thoughts, beliefs, and messages we send to our subconscious to live in harmony and not conflict. It is time to realize we create based on our appetite for life. Change the diet of your thoughts, check out your beliefs, and monitor your actions and reactions to the stuff of life. The pace of life can be extreme. Seek the lessons of form brought about by the use of meditation, contemplation, and prayer. When the life force is strong, do not rely solely on strength and force. Instead, seek the gentleness of spirit and the cultivation of your energy to bring about good works for yourself, your community, and humanity. The way of the future is to realize the opportunity that you possess as a life force.

Contemplation of the forms of life leads one to a greater sense of the magnificence of nature and the role we play as a life force on Earth. The way of contemplation requests your presence. It requests your focus on a subject of your choosing. The contemplation of something you see every day may invoke in your awareness the beauty of its underlying cause and the forces of nature at play—the wings of a bird in flight, the colors on the wings of the monarch butterfly, the movement of water as it flows gently over rocks in a stream. The list is endless. Give your mind, body, and essence a chance to unite in a comfortable place that will provide you respite from the clamor of modern society. The way of life is through life that seeks harmony and potential. The beginning may be easy for some and a challenge for others. Either way, allow your inner nature to guide you.

Pause in your daily routine to ask the following question: "What is it that makes me think I am [insert your name here]?" Use just your first name. If you have a nickname, you can use that. Use whatever name you feel is yours. The focus of this exercise is to get you to broaden your image of what you currently accept without consciously thinking about it.

I want to highlight activities, beliefs, and the working patterns of your thoughts and actions. I am focusing on the normal and mundane aspects of life. It is the day-to-day mechanism that allows the current trends of creation to continue for you. The focus is awareness, not judgment, fear, or guilt. The focus is on understanding so that through awareness, we can bring about a change for humanity and the individual light that will blend together and create what has never been created before: a world of harmony through unity.

The state of man appears to be in decline because of the use of devices that stimulate and make the imagined more intense. The focus of the time is on distraction, when it is imperative that the time calls for greater understanding of self and self-identification in relation to group dynamics. This group is not identified by anything you perceive as different or separate in any way. The form of identification today is with labels. *I am* is a distinction. It is a separator in human terms. *We are* is an accumulation of identities with a broader appeal. What a unique concept it is when *We are* becomes *I am* as a community of human beings with the goal of advancement for all. It's a utopian notion maybe, but the time for man to raise to the level of his potential has just begun. It starts with a concept, and if not used for self-serving purposes, it becomes a catalyst for ideas, actions, and potential for the future. One that creates the dynamic for mankind to gain greater access to the realm where we are connected in a way we never thought possible.

My message is to be open to the infinite possibilities of creation and to the miracles of the heart. The possibilities of creation reside in the Infinite Mind of All There Is. What does that mean? It means that the limits you have created for yourself are imaginary. The thoughts and beliefs we hold are based on the vibration of the patterns of reality that we accept, not on the true capacity that is there for us to explore. The Infinite Mind of Creation took us from the horse and buggy to the automobile and jet plane of today. The Infinite Mind of Creation took us from the darkness of caves to the smart homes of today. When we use knowledge for things other than a higher calling, we can find new ways to destroy one another. The Infinite Mind of Creation allows access to knowledge. What we do with that knowledge defines us. I do not pretend to know why we have been given the ability to destroy one another. The Infinite Mind of Creation is there for us to use. It is our birthright to create and express our unique aspects of life eternal. We have to understand life is for us to realize the true cause of our creation. The true nature of what we are capable of when we understand the role we are meant to play. We can continue to wander before the veils that keep us from our true destiny or we can begin to perceive life as it is truly meant to be lived. One where peace it not a word that is based on wishful thinking but is actualized in every one of us.

Miracles of the Heart

When it comes to the miracles of the heart, the expansion of our capacity to love and nourish is without limits. The universe we exist in is a miracle. It provides us with an ability not only to receive miracles but also to be a part of miracles now and forever. What is the light when it comes to miracles? The light is the defining element of spirit and action. The light of miracles is the changing of life directions. Miracles seem so rare that when miracles occur, they are doubted. People say, "It was coincidence," or "The person was not really cured or sick," or "It's temporary; things will go back to the way they were." Or we bend our knees in prayer at such a holy event. We are miracles; we just don't know or acknowledge it. Check your breathing someday. How long will you consciously be aware of your breathing? For most of us, the awareness lasts a minute or two at best. How about your five senses? Have you ever paid attention to your registering of sight, sound, touch, taste, or smell? Not for long, I would guess. These things are taken for granted unless one or more senses are not available to us. Then there is an effort to replace those senses with greater attention on our other senses.

The miracle of our heart is a journey through science, religion, and technology. It is a journey of faith and good karma. The flight of one's mind states that the heart is an organ that cannot be replaced. It can beat outside the body, and it can be stopped and started again. The heart can, in a sense, attack when something goes wrong. Doctors have even given that phenomenon a name: heart attack.

None of our other organs has that designation in mass consciousness when something goes wrong. A person who has a loving nature has an open heart. A person who is bitter and unfriendly has a hard heart. When one finds love for the first time, the heart is full. The heart even has a symbol: ♥. The symbol of love is closely identified with the heart.

So what is the miracle of the heart? It is the full expression of the truth of your being in a state of grace. When miracles occur, the expression of the heart is blessed. This does not refer just to big miracles, such as a person with cancer being instantaneously cured or a person receiving a kidney right before their time runs out. It refers to little miracles as well. All miracles, big or small, come from the Source of forgiveness and grace, which makes them gifts of beauty. Small, seemingly innocent miracles include not moving forward on a green light as a speeding car goes through a red light at an intersection or not being on the 111th floor of the World Trade Center on the day it was hit by a jet plane. Personal note: I was to attend a business dinner that Friday evening on the 111th floor of the World Trade Center.

The miracle of miracles is that they are part of our journey so that we may know from others or from our own personal experience that they exist. This knowledge is of importance when it comes to faith in the results gained by someone who has faith and allows it to guide him or her. If used properly, it's a template for a new beginning, one not just for the miracle recipient but also for those who are aware of its occurrence. In many cases, it gives someone a new lease on life. An opportunity to contribute to not only their growth but others, as well.

Miracles allow all of us an opportunity to realize that there is something beyond what we can see, feel and hear. It is a demonstration of creativity where harmony and unity come together to create and manifest in an act of grace. We are all capable of miracles when we reach within for a true understanding of the fundamental idea that we are more than the image we currently accept.

Cygnus Light

The Stream Continues

The light that came from the constellation of Cygnus was filled with an energy that was of a greater concentration of life source particles than what we normally receive from the sun. The light that arrived from the constellation of Cygnus is based in a form that allows for penetration into conscious application of thought and expression. The role of this light is to move man off of the existing patterns of knowledge-based beliefs that we have in the third-dimension. The focus and form of light meld together to increase one's ability to (1) hold light and (2) express light. This will have a twofold effect. First, those who seek light will more readily find it, and second, those who deny its expression and potential will continue to experience life as their beliefs dictate.

The light from the constellation Cygnus leaves no physical trace based on man's limited perception of the spectrum of light. The light is a product of an intelligence that radiates outward in the free-flow form of space. The way mankind receives the stream of light is the way knowledge is transmitted throughout the universe. Conscious application of the light stream is here to receive now.

Form and content merge in the absolute field of higher intelligence. What does this look like? That which follows is the beginning of transition from doubt and fear to the realm of reality thinking. Intelligence is seen as a product of mind, when in reality, it is the result of complex combinations of energies. This is not a science lesson. It is, however, the discourse on human evolution. The mind of man is a receiver. It is a director of complex patterns that allow for the thinking process to take place. The realm of thought is not above or below in nature. It is a constant, for the field of thought not only occupies dimensions but also dwells within the molecules of creative certainty. This field is an absolute reality in the confines of creative knowledge and wisdom. What one hears, feels, and experiences dwells in this field. What differentiates one person from another is how well equipped one is to receive and formulate the ingredients of this field. It is not that one is better than another, but the capacity, willingness, and positioning of a life force to extrapolate the energies as information differentiate one being from another.

The other aspect of intelligence is based on the time, place, and space that one is incarnated into. Progression of consciousness allows the field to be reviewed with more clarity in relation to one's life journey. The stage of evolution seems to apply so-called modern concepts to one's existence. That which was horse and buggy yesterday is seen as jet planes today and self-driving vehicles tomorrow. The time does not matter to the human brain. What does matter is how thought is applied to current situations. The way of now is currently littered with obsolete ideas and beliefs. The focus is on the current way of processing information so that mankind can grasp the issues at hand. The reason for greater clarity is to allow for awareness of the current time to precede the flow of knowledge. That is the point of clarity when working with the Cygnus light.

Progress now is available to those who choose or seek a better solution to the world's identity. What is going on is an evolution of thought. Driving this evolution are the cycles and rhythms embedded in the force of movement. What is taking place is the result of an opportunity to access the form and content of life that has been somewhat shrouded or ignored by man's focus on things of little substance. This is not judgment; this is stated as fact on the levels that mankind currently occupies. Move into a relationship with divine forces, and that which is currently hidden is revealed. It does not matter how you see yourself or what your current designation in life is; that which is truly heart directed brings clarity, if one is open to the truth.

Once mankind moves from the realm of self-deception to a place of focused resolve, the heart will not only follow but also direct.

Light is the direction of the moment. One does not realize we are the future of All There Is in this moment. If all of mankind would just for a second seek truth, the veils would fall, and the light of a greater reality would reveal itself.

There is a requirement for more of mankind to be a generator of goodwill, because that is what is called for at this moment in time. The process of evolving thought is based on availability—availability in the form of receptivity and awareness in the content and directions of ideas and actions. Once mankind moves to a point of receptivity of higher consciousness, the movement toward the healing of self, group, and mass consciousness will present itself. This never has been truer than at this time. A movement of goodwill through the power of love will allow greater usage of the field of intelligence. I call this field the potential of infinite possibilities.

How appropriate it is that the field of infinite possibilities is in the person who pursues his or her greatest dreams. It states that all things are possible. Then why the lack and limits of humanity? Why do we not all have the world at our feet?

Did you wake this morning to a new sunrise with the expectation that you could and would have anything you desired? Did you spring out of your bed or place of slumber and know without a doubt or fear that you would be safe and well fed and have everything go your way? All day, did you express yourself in the way you felt? Did you move through the day without judgment of yourself and others? If the answer is yes, you are not only blessed; you are a ray of sunshine on the landscape of human consciousness. If the answer is no, if people are truly honest with themselves, most would answer no to most of the questions, if not all of them—then doubt, fear, judgment, and self-denial are the foundation for the day you experience. There is more to it, such as cause and effect, but I will focus on the opportunity, not the history.

The field of intelligence waits. Now, in this moment, the mind of man processes that which is known, that which is desired, and that which is accepted through belief. In this moment, the opportunity to explore the infinite is available.

Love one another. It is an opportunity. Take this opportunity to love one another. "Why did you insert that thought here?" one might ask. Because the time of love is endless. If you take a moment to love yourself, you love all there is. This is not provable based on current consciousness levels. What is provable is the thought of love, as well as your internal chemistry. It is provable scientifically. If that is the case, why don't we love ourselves?

What does it take to love oneself? There is within us a blueprint that can bring forth a dynamic of life we refer to as love. The source of that dynamic is beyond the use of words and our limited thoughts. When we direct that dynamic outward, there is a sense of upliftment and of release. When we direct that dynamic inward, it requires acceptance. How can we accept love when we see ourselves as unworthy? What is within us that will not accept love? It is an aspect of self-denial. There is a path through the wildness that leads us to love, if we become aware of the limits we have placed on ourselves.

What form does love take in your life? The inner workings of man and his kind dwell in a region of reality that has given love a shallow range of emotion. Love is thought of as chemical or emotional. Love is not perceived for its true nature. Love is the action of life itself. Love is a breath, and love is the blink of an eye. Love is a flower in bloom, and love is a leaf as it falls to the ground. Love opens one's eyes in the morning and closes them in physical death. To love themselves, people have to respect the creation that they are and the Creator who shared with them the ability to experience and express life.

The Light Within

All of creation has a guiding light. The story of the three wise men is a story of light providing the direction to a new birth, a new state of consciousness for mankind. The story of the North Star is seen as a fable to some and a fact of history to others. This is the moment of another star providing the light of a new direction, a new birth. The direction and birth are not of one man's journey that brought us to a new level of consciousness but to mankind's awakening to the potential of creation.

This is a crossroads between the state of existence that is now considered real and the moment when the dynamics of evolutionary forces are now identified and accepted. The crossroads exists to provide a form of choice—the choice of reduced consciousness in its present form or expanded consciousness based on the awareness that the current model of perception and existence is not sustainable.

The light that guides the direction forward with an open mind is bright to those who seek a greater participation in life's gifts. This light is indwelling, seeking acceptance and availability. The light I speak of is free to all of mankind. It does not favor one versus another. It does not choose; it is chosen. The way forward is illuminated by this light. What are its requirements? The one who chooses light does so voluntarily. No fear is attached to the choice. The level of current awareness does not matter. What does matter is a willingness to be open, fair, honest, and kind. The light is not restrictive, so it does not dwell in judgment. The light I speak of has a language, so it seeks those who are willing to learn. The light belongs to no one, so it cannot be possessed. Once the light is accepted, it does not reveal all through the conversion of men. It allows the truth to be identified by direct experience. There is no ritual associated with the light, for it shines brightly on all occasions.

The light of knowledge within the realm of conscious thought is rather dim at this juncture in time and space. The reason this is so is not apparent to the average person on Earth. There are very few who at the present moment are able to judge the brilliance or lack of brilliance of the light of knowledge at this time. It is not an understatement to say that the light within mankind can be increased. As the universal flow of mankind through the yugas[7] has taken place, light is manifested in consciousness to either a greater or lesser degree. The current flow is in Dwapara Yuga, which means we are moving toward a greater awareness of the light within us. The magic of evolution is that nothing stays the same. People, plants, oceans, mountains—nothing stays the same. As we move on, the situation we find ourselves in provides us with an opportunity. We can choose to stay in our current focus in life or strive for a greater sense of purpose. This is the moment to create using the awareness of movement.

If everything in life is moving, why does our focus on life stay somewhat rigid? Why does our conscious habit of thought and perception stay within a narrow range? Part of the answer is due to our tendency to function based on association. Our mind holds patterns that we think of as memory. When a new thought or situation takes place, we go to existing patterns to create an association of something we already know or have experienced. We seemed to be programmed to accept what falls within the range of our current concepts of reality. Based on our beliefs and patterns of reality, this can be restricting as we move forward in life.

---

[7] Yugas are the four ages of a Hindu world cycle. The four yugas are Kali Yuga, Dwapara Yuga, Treta Yuga, and Satyu Yuga. A cycle is twelve thousand years.

If you are seated or lying down, I suggest you stand up while reading this material. Now, if you have room, take a step. Which foot did you use, and why? When you brushed your teeth this morning (I hope you had time to), which hand did you use? When you got out of bed, what was the first thing you did, and why? When you read an article about a child in dire circumstances, what is your reaction, and why? When you exercise, what is your purpose for exercising, and what exercise is most comfortable for you? Why?

The habit, routine, and reason are linked to an inner calling based on a certain comfort factor. It is based on habit, even though things around you have changed. You persist in moving and doing things in a way that holds your conscious effort in a narrow pattern of comfort and familiarity. I understand that in war-torn, highly volatile, highly threatening areas of this world, the term *comfort* seems misplaced. I agree to a certain extent, but I know that certain patterns of reality are confined to a narrow range, especially those that threaten one's survival. Mankind does not move to higher ground because of the current level of awareness. The judgment of the current state of affairs is not the focus of this material. What currently is taking place is the result of a concept of life that has led to extremes. These extremes are based on a lack of understanding of life's gifts. It is time for evolutionary changes to bring forth a rediscovered level of knowledge that will allow for the forces of extremes to reexamine their use of beliefs and thoughts to justify their actions.

A majority of human beings appear on the surface to seek harmony and peace in their lives. Why do extremes seem to dominate the landscape of present-day Earth? The truth lies in the levels of belief mankind uses as his road through existence. The world is seen as separate, and one has a sense of isolation even in a crowd. The world of man can turn extreme in an instant. One must be prepared for that which is unknown. The darkness of life is not just a belief; it is seen and experienced in one form or another as reality. The news of today reinforces this concept of life continually. The history books and records state this is fact. The existing norm is one of upset, difficulty, or challenge after another. This is life on Earth. We must ask why, and what can we do about?

We ask that you remember, the title of this section is "Some Things to Think About."

Second Wisdom Stratum

L istening to your heart seems simple, but how often do you do it?
The heart is here for you. Can you say the same?
Love is a four-letter word.
The result of loving intent is wordless.

Section 3

A Way Forward

Completion

The way forward is not without obstacles. The way is littered with unfulfilled dreams, stories of sorrow and loss, and a lack of understanding of what it means to be human. The nature of reality is like a book of heroism, courage, compassion, self-sacrifice, conflict, cruelty, intolerance, self-destruction, isolation, and hardship. The question of "Why me?" has been repeated throughout time. What does one say to a life filled with scarcity, pain, and suffering? What does Earth hold, if not conflict, loss, and destruction? The balance of life always seems to weigh on the side of the strong, forceful, or just plain fortunate. What does the future hold if we persist on our present course?

Let us not look at the present moment as representative of the future of man. Instead, let us look for a stream of consciousness that sets a new course. The opportunity is here, but the requirement is new in terms of consciousness and direction. The way to the old ways is closed. Our focus on this stream of consciousness requires a different set of parameters. The way to the future lies in the current moment of transition. Speaking the words of past remembrances continues the vibration of what was. The list of what one remembers is endless. The focus of a new sunrise requires a realignment of thought and ideals. The beliefs of a time gone by are resulting in today's experience. The focus going forward is not extreme or difficult. It will take faith and trust, but the result will reveal itself in a short period of time. Focus on conscious reality, not in a dream but in a state of awareness. The desire to achieve greater harmony is of importance not just to each person but also to the collective that holds the consciousness of man.

How do you get from here to there? How do you begin a journey when you don't know your destination? How do you ready yourself once you decide this is a journey you wish to take? The answer is that you are already on the journey you believe takes you through life. You do not know your destination, but you follow your beliefs, and the patterns of reality you see as real to go through life. You have prepared yourself based on your physical, emotional, and mental makeup. If you believe in divine guidance, you follow the path of spiritual guidance and, for many, service. If you follow a radical, or extreme, sense of purpose, you follow what you believe is truth. The combinations of life are beyond description, but know that you follow a path based on what you believe gave rise to your birth. There is no wrong or right, just the manifestation of the energy of your inherent beliefs. The window of your soul dictates a certain outlook, and you bear witness to its direction. The light at the end of the tunnel is the light of the expression you choose to be in this world.

I have titled this section "Completion" because the completion of one's inner drama is at hand. The chance to turn and face the light with a greater degree of certainty is part of this process. This light is not a light of illumination. It is a light of revelation. Some will think this is an exaggeration, but I will attempt to demonstrate the truth of this statement.

Light is the product of energy. All energy has a source. The energy of thought is inherent in the minds and hearts of man. The energy of creation comes from thought. The thought of creation comes from an infinite source. Try going without thought for a while. The truth of thought is that it is endless. There was a beginning to your thought as a being of Earth. There will be a thought as you transition from Earth. The main difference will be that you believe thought begins in the human brain. The question is this: What happens when you are no longer in physical form? How do you process thought then? The answer comes from the source of all thought within the Infinite Mind of Creation.

Now I ask you to reflect on thought and energy. What do you do with your thoughts, and how do you use your energy? We are still focused on the light at the end of the tunnel. Ask yourself the following questions if you are so inclined: What is the nature of your thoughts? Are they angry, sad, happy, or indifferent thoughts? Are they loving, hateful, limiting, or optimistic thoughts? Do you flow from thoughts that are positive to thoughts that you realize are negative?

Will you sit down and write what your thoughts are? It would be a good exercise if for no other reason than to become more aware of the thoughts forming the patterns of your life. I ask that you try not to judge your thoughts as good or bad, but I do ask that you just observe. To do battle with thoughts you deem unworthy is a game that is difficult to win. Remember, thoughts are energy. When you set up resistance to a thought, you have just added to the energy patterns you have within. One approach is to try to become an observer. Being in a state of awareness allows you to gain a better sense of what is taking place. By your doing so, the energy and emotions of the thoughts you are feeling that are the basis for negative results in your life will, if you are patient, begin to lose focus and dissipate. But you should be vigilant. The energy is funded from a source you call you, and there is no quick fix other than your attention and awareness. I suggest you create an intention that lifts up your energy when you are aware of the tape being played out in your mind and emotions that you sense is moving your energy to a place of negativity that does not bring you joy.

The focus of today is the light you allow as you move through the labyrinth of your desires. The one light that guides you guides all of mankind. The question is this: Why does that light seem to shine for some and not for others? The firmament is filled with the brightness of suns and stars. There are differing degrees of brightness throughout the universes. What is the basis for light so that some will shine more brightly than others? The simple answer is energy, but that leaves out a myriad of causes for the brightest of stars versus the dimmest. There is a profound saying: "As above, so below." The reflection of stars in the firmament and the reflection of light here on Earth follow similar patterns of creation. There is nothing that does not follow creation's plan. The light within each and every one of us follows creation's plan. So why is the light brighter in some than in others?

Light is the energy of life. Light is not a reflection of the Source; it is a demonstration of the Source. Light is the power of life. It is a force of the creation that abides within. Each and every one has a force of light within. The demonstration is seemingly absent from some and not others because of the karmic journey one is on. The form and content of life are seemingly without end. Therefore, the amount of light present is based on one's will to demonstrate the essence of creation one possesses. The stage of life is a drama. What part one chooses to play is unique to each individual. Can you change the role you have chosen, or can you change your habits and thoughts? The answer to both is yes. You can change because you have been given a great gift. That gift is your ability to go beyond the habits and beliefs you have held for as many years as you can remember. You not only can change, but you can do so by increasing your awareness and the capacity of the thoughts and beliefs you possess. You can lift yourself up by the quality of your desire to pursue a life filled with the potential of unlimited possibilities. Alignment with gifts of creation requires the focus you possess. When you open a door, you allow something or someone in. Open the door now to your own creative gifts, and see what being in the moment of now means.

The time you take to be a part of life is not wasted. Your actions, thoughts, and beliefs are recorded in the Infinite Mind of Creation. Each moment of each day, you have been given the gift of creation, not just the creation of offspring's but also the creation of mind. You are an infinite source of ideas, thoughts, and opinions. You are an infinite source of action and inaction. The life of one is the interconnection with all of man. No one is separate from his or her connectivity to the truth. No man is an island. We are all the unique expression of creation. No man is less than or more than the totality of life. What people do with the sacred gift of life is up to them and in the direction they have chosen to travel. Now individuals have an opportunity to discover the essence of the world they possess. They can discover that the truth of their birth is what has led them to use the gifts of life in the way they have chosen. The combination of one person's fate versus someone else's is the result of the forces of attraction. The forces of energy expended in thought, belief, and action are the result of what came before. Trusting fate is an abstract. It is the release of responsibility of your creative power. It is a lack of knowledge that you have accepted as a substitute for truth. You choose the path of your destiny, and you are the source of its completion. That statement might be unsettling to some and reaffirming to others. The truth lies in the energetics of life.

The light that is visible now is only a tiny spectrum of the light available to conscious thought. The light of infinite knowledge is seen through the lens of the heart-mind connection. The light of one's creation is based on this heart-mind connection. When one's mind is the predominant aspect of one's capabilities in life, the balance of thought is fixed on facts, opinions, and beliefs, both real and imagined. When one's life is heart based, the ideals of service and nurturing are dominant. When the mind and heart flow back and forth, you get a mixture of both aspects of creation. The mind and the heart serve a purpose: one that is beyond what we currently understand. The challenge for modern man is to focus his ideals in a combination that satisfies not only personal growth but also humanity's growth.

The time to realize a greater truth is at hand. The moment of finite remembrance of the matrix of life is here. Mankind is a member of the creative whole. We are part of something, not apart from the life stream we were and are existing in. The moment of identification will, of its own course of nature, change. We are part of the consciousness of mankind, not a separate piece of life that flows without conscious awareness of the greater whole.

Lift your mind and heart to a place where you can realize that you are more, have been more, and will be more than you thought possible. Light your mind with the prayer of St. Francis:

LORD, make me an instrument of Your Peace

Where there is hatred, let me sow love.

Where there is injury, pardon.

Where there is doubt, faith.

Where there is despair, hope.

Where there is darkness, light.

And where there is sadness, joy.

The prayer goes on, but I will stop here to reflect on what this prayer is stating. Each of us has the ability, when the heart-mind connection is focused as one, to make a difference in the world. Think for a moment. If all of our ideals were set on love, pardon, faith, hope, light, and joy, what a world this could be. There is something of importance to realize: the world we exist in is set in duality. St. Francis's prayer gives us a glimpse into this dynamic and a course of action to provide a ray of sunshine into what he perceived as difficult situations.

The completion of the journey is like any journey; it leads to a new sense that there is more to see and more to do. That is indeed the situation with this journey. The first step is to realize that which exists today. The next step is to realize that you play and contribute to what currently exists. The third step is to point out the issues that have contributed to the current conscious levels being demonstrated. The fourth step is to bring out tools to assist in going through change. The fifth step is to release the old ways of conscious existence. The sixth step is to present a vision of what can be, based on the infinite possibilities within us. Throughout the material in this book, I will touch on various aspects of the steps that have been listed here.

The future is a vision of the right use of creative thought. It is possible for the divine in us all to be realized. We have just begun, but the future awaits us. Let us prepare today and realize our potential for the creative within us. Together we can create a harmonious world. Separately, we create a world where discord is experienced. The choice is not only ours; it is our birthright to bring forth the light of knowledge, wisdom, and truth.

The Way Forward Now

What would it be like if we were to have a moment where we felt united with our creative abilities? No thought of failure, limits or concerns about what others might think. In this moment is joy—the joy of creating. In this moment, there is potential. This is the potential of nature in full bloom. The light of things shines on this moment of joy and potential without any constraints. There are no restrictions in this moment of now. The possibilities are unlimited now with joy as the foundation. It is a focus of the absolute within oneself manifesting in a world awaiting the arrival of one's creativity. How unique is the space individuals reside in as they express their creativity? We are creative beings. What we express is on display for all to see. How much of our expression in life comes from the fulness of joy?

The absolute ability to create is a fixture within the framework of man and his kind. The fundamental knowledge is not apparent without awareness of the facts of one's birthright. What is a birthright? It is that which is inherent in the spark of divine essence that became a living force in the universe—that holy self of divine intent that was gifted with life. One has the birthright to prevail in all endeavors that are in alignment with one's higher calling. What can we do with this information when life is lived as a being subjected to the laws and beliefs of man?

We can sympathize with the plight of man on all continents of Earth, but the truth is not that simple. You see, mankind and his wanderings through the fields of third-dimensional thought and beliefs have created what takes place in our world. The truth is that the world's challenges, when looked at from above, are opportunities for souls to grow in knowledge, wisdom, and stature. The end of existence is not the end of growth. Life is lived on many levels, and the life of this time and place is to realize the fundamental truth that comes forth from this illusion. Your responsibility to create is not alleviated by the statement that this is an illusion. Illusion it may be, but we are still here for a reason. There may be even more than one reason you have come to this experience. The lessons of life may be hard and seemingly without justice, but I assure you the universal plan has us in it; otherwise, we would not be here.

The cause of existence is too voluminous to address here. It is beyond the scope of this journey. The truth of your birth is within the framework of who you are. The reason you are here has been demonstrated throughout your current existence. The ways and means may not be apparent, but they are here in what you do and how you do it. Focusing now on the future requires your attention. It also requires your receptivity. The life span of one person is different from the life span of another based on the lessons and cycles of life one is to go through. The formula is a combination that science has yet to address. The underlying cause of existence based on our present journey is not easy to comprehend. The reason for our experience is that the cycles of refinement are presently increasing in intensity. The level of vibration within the earth, air, fire and water is increasing. The water planet of Earth has experienced and is experiencing expansion as the ice sheets melt. The melting appears to be due to global warming, which is the result of the cycles within time, space, and place. The current state of evolution of mind, technology, science, and education leads one to continue the belief in external forces. The reality is that the forms of creation are in perfect alignment with the vibration within the cycles now being experienced.

Fear is the opposite of the expansion now taking place. When fear is employed, there is a weakening of structure and of intent. When faith and trust are demonstrated, there is expansion or an opening in a closed system. This means you are asked to have faith and trust in the future by employing the knowledge that you are an integral part of creation. You have abilities that can conquer all the limits you have instilled in your conscious and subconscious mind. With knowledge, you can be more, not less, of a participant in life. I welcome your acceptance in this venture. It is time to move on together.

The rest of the journey requires that your awareness be focused not on the past or future but on the present. How is this possible when so many things take place and you have so many obligations or interests? The current moment is a way for you to clear space and open yourself to the infinite possibilities of life. How do you do that when your journey has been filled with the things of life? The moment you consciously take a breath, you have arrived at a place of conscious intent. The taking of a breath is symbolic. Make up your mind to receive the light of conscious awareness: "I AM a being with the strength to go in the direction of my heart." It's simple and straightforward. That is the journey you are on. The noise of life is your lesson. The strength of your conviction to be present represents the direction of your steps. Once you understand or appreciate the strength of your indwelling self, your journey in life will be clearer.

The opening of consciousness is not an accident. There is some aspect within you that seeks not only clarification but also insight into the cause and purpose of your life. The indwelling spirit that you are seeks your awareness, for without your awareness, you will continue your journey without the insight required of you to succeed. This is not to indicate that you are a failure or to dismiss your accomplishments to date. On the contrary, you have succeeded in doing all or most of what you have set out to accomplish. This material is about an awareness that raises your consciousness up to a level that is in accord with the times of this rhythm and cycle.

I ask that you open your mind and heart to realize the change you are part of. We are all part of the change that is taking place. I ask that you not take this in any way as a fear-based statement.

It is meant to raise your awareness so that your focus is on your potential and the potential of the world around you. Life is alive. Life is dynamic. Life is a celebration of your participation. How you register your relation to the life within you and the world is how you function in it. The mystery of life is that most human beings not only take it for granted but also minimize their roles in it. Life is light as a dynamic covered in the guise of nature. Your role is to open your eyes anew and hear with a greater intensity. Clear the space between your ears, and begin with a sense of purpose to follow your heart.

Most of what is being given is blessed by your awareness and participation. You are the holder of the key of life—not that you are alone in this endeavor. Each man, woman, and child hold the key to the truth of his or her higher nature. That key is not just knowledge and wisdom; it is love. It is a love that cannot be described by the words on this page—infinite, radiating love. These words still do not reflect the purity I refer to. Make this a goal: once you realize you are the key, do not stop your process until all you see is love. When I began this journey through the labyrinth of the Emergence I heard, "Start with truth and do not stop until all you see is love".

The time of transition speaks to effort. What type of effort am I referring to? The willingness to give life, your life, a chance to expand its potential and to be open to concepts and knowledge that might make your efforts and role in life more rewarding. Your willingness might allow you to see the greater possibilities in and of life. Sow now your seeds for a new harvest. Each year, farmers around the world plant seeds, hoping for the abundance of nature. As one sows the seeds in faith, so too does the natural flow bring forth the harvest. I ask simply that you listen to the messages being shared here. The agenda is for humanity to grow as a citizen of the celestial realm; realize the oneness of their creation; and, through unity and commonality of purpose, bring forth the rewards of harmony and peace.

The form and content of man remains focused on the opposites of life as lessons to be learned. What does mankind do when form and content are subject to pressure? In many cases, the loss of the form and content that abide externally means they are replaced by other forms and content that provide similar comfort. This appears to refer to the material things of life. The replacement of form and content involves using habits and creative thinking to replace the original items in our world. The capacity to replace and seemingly make new is just a small part of our creative abilities. The world will soon require the replacement of form and content for many. There is a moment in which you can realize the gift of creation on a new level. This moment flows through this material in unique and distinctive ways. One has to be open to the messages within this information to realize its importance.

Not all of life is as it appears. The vehicle of one's life seems to change as the years fly by. The consciousness that one possesses seems to grow based on experience, but the sense of one's life essence appears the same. This is true on the level of conscious thought and participation in life. The way forward appears as a challenge of continuity. How can things around you change, while you appear to your conscious essence as the same? The true you is a life stream of conscious essence. It is pure and untouched by the role you have taken, for it is your observer. It gets lost in the veil of illusion and the veil of ignorance now and then (or so it seems), but in reality, it is always there. The focus of your being is to bring you to a point where you realize the greatest truth. The creative essence that you are is a reflection of divine sonship. Proving this is a challenge because of the intensity of our acceptance of the illusion that we are separate. The proof is in those ascended beings who have come before us and achieved not only enlightenment but also the self-realization that All is One. It is never separated or divided. It is One.

Now we journey forth to attempt to share greater knowledge and insight that words can only provide a direction to. Here now is insight from divine sources:

- Let the light you are reflect your integrity to demonstrate truth.
- Know you are not alone and have never been alone.
- See your journey as one of courage and fortitude.

- Mark time by being aware.
- Listen to the rhythm of your heart night and day.
- Speak with thought regarding all beings on Earth.
- See with no judgment, and label no one without understanding his or her journey.
- Seek within the inner spark that ignites your consciousness.
- Tell no one that you are above or below him or her. The garden of creation treats all equally.
- See with your heart that all men, women, and children are your brothers and sisters. Leave the dysfunction of your childhood in a place of love.

The light that now guides the flow of words and consciousness changes to adapt to a new tomorrow. The time of accelerated change appears before you as a light of opportunity. The Light of Lights that now guides mankind's destiny does so with a specific destination in mind. The role of the infinite plays a rhythm that requires the time to be seen as a chance to break away from past reality and dwell in the rhythm of now. Focus on the goal of raising mankind's vision of his role in the cycles of nature and the cycles of the celestial mandate called evolution. Take one step in life, and see it is not without purpose. The purpose of now in time and space is to awaken mankind to his role as an active participant in his evolution and, thus, his future.

The time of the now is filled with energy and force that can propel mankind into an age of darkening concepts or one where the light of a greater reality exists. For the moment, time and space pause as if in anticipation of something about to take place. This moment reveals the truth of holding on to worn-out illusion and repeating the false beliefs of bygone eras. The past holds better memories than the future. This is a realm of regret: "I wish I would've done this instead of that. I wish I could have. I should have. If I had to do it over again, I would." Now comes the ideal moment to realize one's truth. You are what you should be based on your thoughts, beliefs, actions, and words. There is no mistake: the road you have taken is the road you are on for a myriad of reasons. All follow the laws of creation in this atmosphere of supposed reality. Now you can feel sorry for yourself or feel good about yourself. Your judgment of this time and space is subject to the beliefs you reflect. They are based on the screen of imagined reality. The time to realize that this moment when you are capable of extraordinary things lies at your feet. The path of your journey toward the light of creation is based on the path you choose. Your remembrance of the light that dwells within can be one of joy and gratitude. The light seeks the way forward as you choose the way forward. Let the moment of your receptivity be now. Choose now consciously to move forward in light.

In a moment of silent contemplation, I heard the following statement, which resonated deeply within my heart and mind. This wisdom statement, appears to reinforce that the light seeks the way forward as you choose the way forward: "God gives to life what life gives to life."

Mark the time as one of optimism and opportunity. Why optimism? There is within each child of creation the joy of exploration and creativity. Why do we see this as a time of opportunity? There is within a capacity for us to change and to realize that we can learn, express, and become the future of mankind. We have the gifts, the spirit, and the courage to move from this place of extremes to a place of harmony. We just have to let in the truth of what is available and what is ours to demonstrate.

Quietly, now open the doors of your mind and heart to that which is herein presented as just one of many paths to the realm of higher expression in divine right thinking and being.

Light Is

The Power of Mind to Create Eternally

The power of mind is a description used to direct one's attention to the mind that indwells creation in form and content. The way to access this level of mind requires the sense of purpose that is driving you to read this material. There is no one you must seek permission from to allow you the right to fulfill your own destiny. The formula for achieving a higher purpose in life comes from your inner desire to achieve a sense of quiet peace that tells you you're on the right path. There are ways to know truth from that which conceals truth. Dr. David R. Hawkins, in his book *Power vs. Force*, goes into the extensive work he did on testing for truth versus nontruth. A friend who owned a metaphysical store told me about a gentleman who came in and proceeded to place several books before his heart. If he moved backward, he put the book back on the shelf. If he moved forward, he purchased the book. I had heard about this technique, which was taught by a tai chi master. Unfortunately, I was never told the *sifu's* name. Another way is to communicate with your heart to find out what is and is not true for you. The way you communicate with the heart is based on your desire to know and live in a realm where truth is not just a goal or ideal but the basis for existence.

The spirit of being holds the key to the mystery of why mankind sees only what is believed and accepted as fact. This is the progression of man from spirit to form to spirit released. The level of ascension is based on the spark of light throughout time. No man goes beyond the light of the spark of his or her creations. Intent drives the vehicle of expression—intent in the form of knowing and in the existence of future endeavors. This is now. The future is in the form of possibilities. It awaits the intent to create. This is now. The form of existence is open to those who seek to identify truth. Truth in knowing, truth in action, and truth in faith are the three levels of future results.

What Are Truth in Knowing, Truth in Action, and Truth in Faith?

That which is truth is an abstract in the creative mind of those who perceive the third dimension as real. When individuals seek truth, they seek that which aligns with their purpose of being and their inner essence. Truth is the destination. The journey of men is to find not only their purpose for being but also their inner essence.

What is truth? It is the focus of life that is bound to achieve totality. It is an understanding that passes all insight, knowledge, and creativity. It is union with creation itself, where distance, time, and focus on the self no longer exist. It is not total absorption, but it is consummation of one's journey. Truth is the ideal from which there is no alternative or option. Only truth exists when there is no distraction.

The word *bound* is not adequate to describe what is given. It is a certainty that totality will be achieved. The attraction of truth is so strong and majestic that one is drawn to it in a way that finding truth is the only thing that matters.

Truth in Knowing

Life is a process. It is an adventure of experience and, ultimately, growth. The search for truth is a search for knowledge. It is the development of a mind-set that seeks until it finds what it is searching for. Truth in knowing is a direction that does not allow for that which is suspect or not proven by direct experience. When one moves toward the moment of enlightened thought, he or she is asked one question: What is the importance of knowledge to you?

Why is this asked as one progresses to a state of understanding that is not restricted by prior concepts of the reality of life? What purpose does knowledge have when it is kept to oneself? Knowing is not doing. Notice that the second aspect of this trinity is truth in action.

Knowing is not just a direction and the limitation of knowledge; it is the direct experience that is wordless. Knowing truth is the result and not the journey to find an alternate level of awareness. What is the process of truth in knowing?

Consciously seeking the truth is a fixed pattern of reality. It is the desire and the persistence to find for oneself what lies beyond the veils of illusion and ignorance. The process is self-alignment with the inner essence that sparks consciousness. Hidden in the depths of what is lies a pattern that generates life's expression. This is a divine blueprint of subtle yet vital energy. The way is the focus, intent, and faith in that which is sought, which is truth—not just the truth that is accepted but also the truth that is realized.

Truth in Action

Action stems from desire. Where does desire come from? It comes from an inner action of consciousness that is above awareness. Action is the result of movement, and movement that aligns with the cycle of the time aids in achieving one's goal. The moment of action is a moment of decision. The decision is generated from a stimulus that is either internally generated or an external result that prompts one to move in a direction of his or her choice. The choice is seen as finer in nature than normal actions.

The way of action toward the truth is set from above. This is a link with the dynamics of soul and conscious awareness that exist in the framework of life. Truth in action is the result of a spontaneous dynamic that is not just soul driven but also personality driven. The time and place of the action of truth are embedded in knowledge that is not earthbound.

Truth in action has results that are not locally experienced. Truth manifests experience, and that experience is not restricted to any locale, region, or country. The truth in action manifests in a way that is experienced at several levels of consciousness. The truth that is the result of one's journey is experience, and that experience leads to outreach and an expression that results in change. What is the process of truth in action?

Live life willfully and with upright purpose. Do not stoop to learn, but stand tall during the journey. Seek only the purity of your action and intent. No one or thing can be accepted when the result is incomplete. The action is heart based, and the mind is set on experiencing what comes next. Each step is seen as part of the journey, and the journey is in the doing. Lift up the eyes to see, and allow the inner core to hear by feeling the vibration of refinement.

Truth in Faith

You are the matrix of a given life. That life is lived through the soul and through the embodiment that is now. How appropriate is it that one opens him or herself to truth? The *sense of faith* is the term for a religious experience. How refined is the spirit of truth? How refined is the spirit of accomplishment in a sense of love? How can we have faith when the truth seems to be out there? Realigning faith so that truth is seen as a concept of totality is appropriate. The faith one has is based on his or her willingness to let go and release the most important possession: the self.

Truth in faith is a result. It is the answer to a prayer and a declaration. When one finds truth, faith is rewarded in a way that transcends words. Faith is an open door, and that door must remain open. One's faith is, in part, one's destiny. It is part of one's reason for being.

Faith is an energy. It is the polishing of one's expectations that truth is greater than the totality of his or her known universe. Faith has the power of a magnet. It attracts levels of reality that is part of the universes both seen and unseen. For truth to respond to faith, it must be given a home, and that home is within the patterns of reality that one creates. This dynamic is one of a singular accomplishment: the relinquishing of self through the understanding that the greatness of life is in the living. It is living in the present moment with a sense of oneness with creation. What is the process of truth in faith?

Center the self on what is greater than what currently exists. See and feel the oneness of being in the moment. Set faith on the action of heart and mind. Allow the spirit of the moment to reside in your heart. Open the mind to what is possible. Open the heart to the greatness of a Universal Spirit that resides within All. Make the time one of respect and openness. Truth does not exist in a vacuum. It exists but on a level that does not reduce life to a happenstance or to irrelevance.

All three aspects of a search for truth are within one's realm of existence. There is now, and there is tomorrow. The search for truth is one in which the intent is clear, but the results are not. By starting a journey to truth, one begins at a place of opportunity. There is within a chance to learn and grow. There is a chance to see and accept changes to one's perception of life. Willingness and openness are called for, as well as a sense that what is available is greater than what is accepted as life in the now. Future results are an open-ended question. When one journeys forth, what is most important or valuable—the steps along the way or the results? This a question for each seeker to answer. One's journey is the goal of a lifetime. How real is that?

The Emergence comes from the inner depths of being. Isolation of thoughts and beliefs are revealed as habits, as patterns of life expectations and resulting experiences. The only way to understand what is taking place is through awareness. The obvious is not so apparent when it is an ingrained pattern of conscious reality. Creation is a result of the depths of beliefs and thoughts manifested as life experiences. The emergence of this life experience is not newborn but an inner pattern that has been accepted as normal. Mankind dwells at the bottom of the well of knowledge. The only recourse is to understand the limits people have accepted and perpetuated. The way forward is one of opportunity. Release the darkness of a lack of awareness by becoming aware of life's possibilities. How do you reframe what is a pattern of accepted norms? By being aware of what your true potential is. I'm defining *potential* as the choice of the existence that one is capable of. Potential is the application of oneself to knowledge.

Potential

When one thinks of potential, he or she thinks of opportunity. The opportunity to do what? The opportunity to explore the reaches of one's ability to create. When one thinks of potential, one thinks of effort. Effort to do what? Effort to bring out the best in oneself and others. When people think of potential, they think of developing beyond their current circumstances in life. What is it that makes individuals think they can improve and learn and expand beyond their current state of existence? The answer lies within the touchpoints of potential. What are the touchpoints of potential? They are

- learning truth,
- experiencing truth, and
- being truth.

Remember, we are existing in the realm of third-dimensional reality. The first lesson we receive is to learn. We go to the school of life to learn the different aspects of what constitutes our existence, including speaking, walking, eating, and the processes of life. If we are able, we learn to read, write, and receive a form of education, both formal and informal. We learn skills and the utilization of our innate abilities. We are in effect learning the truths of life without realize the true nature and structure of what is taking place. We learn to expand our consciousness through knowledge.

As we grow, we utilize what we learn and are learning to participate in life. We increase our education and, in the process, express what we are learning. We are dwelling in the realm of life, and we find ways to use our knowledge to exist in the world. We enhance our skills, and we advance in the world as we mature. Our experiences of life are used in one form or another to participate in the world around us. For those who learn and pursue their vocations, they move into greater levels of responsibility and share their knowledge with others. We are in effect experiencing and sharing the truths of life. Whatever level of knowledge is acquired, there is a natural tendency to share it. By doing so, you are expressing what you have learned and experienced.

Without regard for status in life, we become in effect what we have learned, what we have experienced, and what our role in life is. We are in essence that which is meant to be. We are the accumulation of our truths at the level of third-dimensional existence.

The issue is this: How far have we come in accepting the limits of our beliefs? How far has mankind come in accepting the beliefs of present and past existence? Potential is a dynamic of resolve. Potential is the mainstream of conscious application of the ability to take an additional step—to try another way or to believe that the moment of now is not a base of possibilities from the past but a creative moment that defines the present and the future.

The concept of restrictions placed on mankind does not take into consideration that everything in nature is in motion. It does not take into consideration that all of mankind is a collective of consciousness who are in the process of learning, receiving, experiencing, and expressing the potential they believe is theirs. What is missing from this scenario is essence. It is what being in this realm is all about. When one learns, experiences, and expresses, he or she is fulfilling the role of a third-dimensional being. The concepts of totality and wholeness are missing. The truth that one sees is not the truth that one is. One is essence. How is that potential?

My light of awareness sees the present and imagines the future. I have accepted the role I played for many years with a sense something was missing. When this information was received, I did not understand everything that was written, and in truth, I am still absorbing the information that is being shared. The question from the prior paragraph becomes the following: What does essence have to do with potential?

The inner calling of man is perceived as spirit. It is perceived as something beyond the grasp of mere mortals. What lights up the sky is above us and not within us. The truth of existence is that all of creation is expressing an inner aspect that seeks the light. It seeks itself. The essence of man is potential both manifest and unmanifest. It is the equilibrium of what is and what can be. Now is a moment of reconciliation, a moment to realize that potential is a desire and inner urge to manifest in accordance with higher laws and higher vistas. It is a time of transition, a time of transitional awareness.

The formula for gaining a greater understanding of self resides in your commitment to learn what the next step on your path is.

Teachers of the Stone

Why did I title this section "Teachers of the Stone"? Many years ago, I started to write a book about love and how to define our purpose in life, but the material was not completed due to personal events and my retirement. However, after all that has and is happening, I am sure I will have to make quite a few changes based on my current experience when I get back to finishing that book. During the writing of that book, I developed sacred-heart-based exercises, and I researched several books about the heart and love. During one of my meditations, or exercises, I thought of the stone that was placed before Christ's burial tomb. When the women went to the tomb, Christ was gone, and the tomb was the scene of his resurrection. At the time of that meditation, I felt I was standing before the cave of my heart. I had the impression I had to roll the stone away from my heart before I could enter. Over the years, I would periodically see the rolling of the stone away from my heart as a way to remind myself of something I was doing or not doing. One morning, while I was working on the material for this book, I was drawn to do the cave-of-the-heart meditation. As I sat quietly, I heard, "The Teachers of the Stone are with you." I immediately saw a large flat stone with two or three beings seated behind the stone. I did not see them clearly, and there could have been more. The direction I received was rather direct but, as I have learned through personal experience, multilayered and expansive. When I started to write this piece, I searched for a moment for the title, and it came to me to call this section "Teachers of the Stone." I will go into this in more detail in the following paragraphs.

The time of accelerated transition is one of uneven events. The nature of man requires some form of continuity. This habitual way of functioning in the world allows for repetition of thoughts and ideals to become ingrained into one's way of thinking. It allows the world to seemingly progress day by day. The absolute rhythm of the universe allows for this type of progressive stream of what appears as reality. The truth of the day seems to change as the truth of tomorrow develops. The greater conceptualization of man is that all things change, but in an order associated with his line of thinking. The reality of man appears based on structure. This structure is indicated by the calendar, which follows the patterns of the sun and the moon. The days are even named for both of them. The ancient calendars of the Chinese and the Egyptians took on a slightly different structure and celestial association. The reason for the dialogue is to orient you to your current way of thinking and beliefs.

The way of the present moment is not as obvious as you choose to believe. Although time and space appear to be accelerating, there is not a connection between current perceptions and the nature of the universe as it proceeds to evolve. The time has come to awaken the light of recognition in as many as hear and see this message. The time of transition speeds to a new horizon to equip mankind with tools to adjust to this time. The adjustment, as stated before, is to the consciousness of change. This a subject for the present moment that requires your attention. This moment is the ongoing momentum of a change in world dynamics. Now there is an opportunity, but this opportunity is subject to the acceptance of world consciousness. World dynamics and consciousness being what they are leads one to believe that as fractured as things seem, there is little chance to bring the world to a state of universal understanding. That is the opportunity of opportunities. All of mankind does not have to have a universal awakening to the realities of the time. Diversity of understanding and of coping with the dynamics of change is not only necessary; it is essential. Because we are at different levels of conscious participation in the third dimension, this indicates that we do not have to all be on the same page in this transition, but we do have to realize that a shift is taking place.

The man of today is not the man of tomorrow. The child of today will certainly not be the child of tomorrow. The woman of today is the strength of today's matrix, and she will not be the same tomorrow. So tomorrow will be different, as will the process of the focus of life. We are still one, but the differences in the infinite path of creation allow and support the function of diversity. The challenges are many, but the one challenge that will create the greatest resistance will be the issue of labels. Labels are the way to differentiate one another. A label is a form of judgment. It is the way we identify one another. If you hang a label on anyone, the person seems stuck with that distinction for a lifetime. One can come up with many examples: one is too fat, short, weak, strong, overbearing, meek, or afraid of success or failure. One is too this or too that. People might be Irish, Chinese, Greek, or Italian, a designation based on where they or their family were born. Being Jewish, Buddhist, Catholic, Muslim, or Hindu is a religious designation. If you stop for a moment and realize the direction of my statements, you begin to realize the labels we place on one another. We are one as members of this planet and our conscious acceptance of life on Earth. We are one as a race of human beings. We are one as the conceptual manifestation of our Creator. We are and will always be one. The issue is simply put: we don't live with that as a reality. We have labeled everything we can think of, and in doing so, we have accepted the concept of separation. Even though we are all unique, the only way to move forward will be as a united *we*. We are the same, and we are one in life and in change. The only difference is the path of creation we choose. That makes us unique and gives us the mass consciousness to evolve. Diversity of expression gives the painter's palette its rich colors, an endless array of colors and hues.

The way of the heart is an interesting subject when it comes to transition. We think of the heart as an organ or the originator of the emotions related to love. People might say, "My heart is full of love for my children," "I love you with all my heart," or "My girlfriend [or boyfriend] broke up with me and broke my heart." You get the idea. The truth is that your heart is much more. It is knowledge and wisdom. When listened to, it will lead you in the right direction. Your heart is the indwelling place of an inexhaustible supply of love. Your heart is a place of clarity when your mind is in a state of confusion. Your heart is the generator of a life stream of consciousness that we have just begun to understand. The more we listen to our hearts, the greater our clarity in life.

The teachers of the stone symbolize at a deep level of consciousness the life-and-death scenario that we built for our experience here on Earth. We are the spirit of being. When we close our heart to who and what we truly are, it is a form of death. When we harden our hearts because of our experiences of the past, we reduce the flow of love's nature to ourselves and others. When we roll the stone over the entrance to the cave of our heart because we want to protect ourselves from further pain, we have placed an object that restricts our ability to love. Harmony and the rhythm of one's personal expression are somewhat confined as a result. Moving the stone is not easy when you do not realize what has happened or the consequences of your actions related to your thoughts and emotions.

The way of the teachers is the way of raising one's consciousness. The time is one of importance. The following visualization is a way to relax, become heart centered, and review the events of the day without judgment: before bedtime, take a moment to just relax and review the events of the day. With no judgment, just watch the day's events. When you lie down to go to sleep, take several gentle breaths. The following cadence helps. Breathe into your lower abdomen to a count of four, hold the breath to a count of four, and release the breath to a count of four. If you are experienced in meditation, yoga, tai chi, or other forms of exercise, you can breathe in to a count of four, hold to a count of four, and release your breath to a count of eight. Do this exercise three times. After the third time, see on the screen of your heart a light that is soft. It can be white, pink, or green. Any other color at this time is not part of this visualization. Just allow this light to illuminate the area around your heart.

It is important to realize that a visualization of this nature is only as good as the effort you put into it. Therefore, I ask that you focus on what has been given. As you view the heart, ask if there is something it wishes to share. If there is no response in less than a minute, move on to the next step. If there is, then note in some way what you are receiving. If it feels right, work with the answer to improve your connection to the heart. Do this by making your consciousness available to the heart as you move through life. If you receive no answer, see yourself presenting a flower of your choice to the heart. My choice is a rose, which represents the feminine flowering of life's love. This is a divine gift when given without expectations both internally and externally. Allow the gift to be laid before the heart, and gently breathe in and out for a minute or two. Allow yourself to enter sleep with the desire to see your heart bloom in accordance with its true nature. The natural tendency will be to fall asleep before you have completed this exercise. If you do fall asleep, then try again the following evening or whenever you normally go to sleep.

After doing this exercise for several nights, the heart should be available to give you some response. Work with those responses to create a line of communication with your heart that can be open both day and night. Know that you may receive not only verbal responses but also images. It is good not to direct the messages. Allow yourself to be receptive without judgment. That is of prime importance. If you feel you are not being given the proper answers, stop the exercise and meditate, not on the answers but on the cause of the seeming disconnect between you and your heart.

The stone before the cave of the heart is more than symbolic. It is the existence of a lesson that is waiting for you to address it. The stone before the cave of the heart could indicate your unwillingness to move on in your life. You are protecting yourself from something, the fear of a prior event is still with you, or you think you are shielding your heart for some reason. The stone is energy in a solid state of creation. It is frozen in time, or so it seems. Because nothing stays the same, the terms *solid state* and *frozen* are used to describe the way the stone is seen and, in some cases, used.

The time of movement of the stone is unique to each person. One, the stone might not be in front of the cave when the heart is already open, and the person is exhibiting this fact through his or her role and relations in life. Two, the stone is there and waiting to be moved. Three, the stone is there, and the person, through his or her beliefs, lives in the past, which can only be described as a form of resistance and stagnation. Four, and this last option is more unique, the stone might exist, but there is such a belief in the darkness of the third dimension's illusion that the stone appears impossible to move without some sort of divine intervention. The cave of the heart is meant to be open. Faith and trust lead one in the direction of what is possible.

The moving of the stone is based on many things, but the one that will be addressed here is faith. *Faith* is a word that has levels that are difficult to describe when sharing what its true unlimited potential is. Faith is usually taken as a positive. In physical form, one can have opposite results related to faith. Through judgment, one selects what is good or bad. In the use of faith, you can have evolution or an upwelling experience or a lowering of vibration. Many of us have placed faith in something or someone that is not productive, such as having faith in people who take what is not theirs or misrepresent who they are and their true motives. I will focus on faith that can potentially move mountains or, in this case, the stone from the cave of the heart.

When faith is placed in a heart longing for truth, the outcome can exceed all expectations. This is the realm of creation where miracles are not only possible but also expected. So what is the key to moving the stone? At the beginning of this piece, I indicated that

I received directions from the teachers of the stone. The following is what I heard: "Faith in heart. Faith in life. Faith in love. Move the stone—now!"

That's it. You might say that does not make sense or appears to be too simple.

It is simple and straightforward for a reason. Faith is not just based on a conscious decision. It is heart generated as well. It does make sense if you understand and give the effort to your desire to move the stone. That is it. Move it not partially but fully as a way to achieve your goal or, in this situation, your heart's desire.

The declaration is "Faith in heart. Faith in life. Faith in love. Move the stone—now!"

You can use the phrases of faith in the order of being in the heart, which is life, and life becomes more dynamic when lived in love, or you can make it your intention to love life from your heart. If you move the trinity into a form of action, the moving of the stone is the reaction of faith and not only in the doing but also in the being—being in the essence of the movement of the heart-mind connection.

I have personally done this meditation using this declaration many times, and it becomes apparent that this leads to levels of understanding and awareness that are both personal and expanding.

The way forward is a test of your faith, the faith of the inner essence that you can connect with. The faith of now in the heart is ascending the ladder of expression. This may seem like a sentence that is without much meaning, but try having or coming from faith within your heart, and I am sure the measure of your steps will change. For many, having faith in life requires a broader approach than their normal way of thinking. Faith in life requires letting go of expectations and allowing the flow of events to take their own course. It requires a broader vision on your part to understand that the role you play is one that you and you alone have created. For many, this will be hard to accept. The faith in love is one of absolute release of what you think love holds for you. It is the reverse of what most people think or believe. Love is a stream of unlimited action. It flows like a river. Have you ever noticed what forms of life exist by the nourishing impact of a river? Love is like a stream when it is allowed to flow. Flowers bloom; life is enhanced. Love is a fundamental element of life. Its secret is that it is never ending and inexhaustible. Give it to someone, and you are filled with its nectar.

When you are focused in a heart filled with faith in life and love, your intention and commitment allow for greater clarity in your life. The seeking of faith is a challenge when doubt has been your constant companion. However, you are blessed with the gift of choice. You can choose doubt or faith. What path would you like before you—one of doubt, which is by its very nature restrictive, or faith which is expansive? As the saying goes, "Faith can move mountains." The choice is yours. The cave of the heart awaits.

The Path

The path of existence is not for a few but for all. That which is exists for a reason beyond all knowledge mankind possesses. The way mankind treads the path of existence is the way all life evolves. No one being is alone on this path. No one being is separate from his or her sole purpose. Each life is a shining star moving through the heavens. This movement is ordained by the momentum of life's consciousness. All beginnings and endings are just a phase of existence. All moments of eternal peace are the reflections of truth as an image of true reality.

The way of the individual is a way of unique expression of will. The way of the individual is a search for that which is lost in some and found in others. The exposure of love's influence is based solely on the desire of the soul. To inherit Earth, mankind had a dream, and the dream became real. Mankind's dream included the stars, sun, and moon. This relationship presented mankind with an opportunity to express creatively in an environment of plenty. The dream of one and the dream of many are the same but seen through the lens of that which is deemed reality. By any name, it is still a dream.

The path of life is, was, and will be a journey of love. How do we know? By the movement and breath of life. Do not mistake this for an idle comment. No man, woman, or child breathes in this dream without love. That is truth. The truth of now is an awakening to the realities that exist within the dream.

Life is an extension of something greater. Each and every path is deemed to be blessed. That each path is the active role of someone is a blessing. That each blessing is alive in a dream is significant. Why do we walk a path that is blessed? Why do we breathe? To live life. Something seems to be missing here. The dream is not real, but it is a blessing. Why? To complete itself. The dream needs to complete itself. Yes and no: yes, to move through the various stages of conscious evolution, and no, to realize that the dream is not the totality of all there is.

Mankind's journey is filled with symbols of life. It is filled with the heartbeat of what was and what will be. The current moment is a bridge to the foundation of the dream. It's a chance, an opportunity to explore the full expression of the creative self. The moment of now is an opportunity to reverse the concept of the term *limits*. It is a point of potential. The path in the dream now provides not what was but what will be and what is about to be. Hold to this ideal. You, I, and we are at the point of unlimited potential. What does that mean?

To begin with, it means no more sorrow or lost opportunity to express the creative self. It means no going back or living in the past. It means hope in a different way. It means no blame for what was or what is. It means total focus on now. There is something very profound underlying this change in the dream that is currently working its way through our desire to express ourselves. The dynamic of our existence is changing and we are asked to change with it.

Judgment in the now is what? I am at the center point of my creation. I stand at this moment before the self I identify as who I am, and I ask for the opportunity to open every door I have allowed to close and stay closed. I could judge myself, but would I listen? I could see the limits I've set upon my path, but I don't know how to release them. I could just sit down and refuse to move forward, but I will only know the harshness of loneliness as all of life progresses around me. How do I move forward when I cannot rely on yesterday? How?

The path of humanity is covered in layers of thoughts and beliefs bound by limitation imposed by our acceptance in illusion. The concept of self is identified in the skin and bones of ancestors. It is a mix of old and new in the way of evolution on a planetary scale. The time of the ego's development happened eons ago, when the dream was accepted. This material is the focus of now. When the time comes, many concepts and beliefs of origination will fall away.

The way forward now seeks to release the old and obsolete concepts of self. The truth of the moment is revealed in the way of the direction of the rising sun. This concept of the rising sun indicates that a new day has begun. Welcome to the light of the vessel that allows you to receive a glimpse into the journey this new day brings. All of mankind sits at a crossroads of the concepts of self-denial and self-liberation. We move ahead through faith, patience, and trust. The faith of a new day requires several things. It requires a willingness to listen. It requires a willingness to learn. It requires a lack of judgment of self and others. It requires the strength and courage to move forward into the seeming unknown and release old habits and beliefs that no longer serve your higher good. It requires that you listen to that inner knowing that change not only is going to come but also is already here.

Focus on what is important in life. That is the goal of life. What is important? The ability to love. You might say, "That cannot be the most important thing in life." Are you sure? For each path, there is a purpose. For each purpose, there is an ideal. For each ideal, there is a definition. Each purpose and ideal is defined by the path of the individual. What is the path of truth? What is the overriding purpose or ideal of humanity? Is it survival? Is it to conquer others? Is it to travel to distant stars? What is humanity's purpose? I have a thought. What if it were to express to the fullest potential of mankind's ability to love? What if it were that direct and simple? How would we change our focus on life, or would we?

At this present level of consciousness, I don't think we would. Therefore, the solution to this situation is to reorient our consciousness and raise the level of our awareness. This is the moment to be aware of the overriding crossroads we have come to. The path is to remember our capacity to love and our ability to use the miracles of creation itself as our guide. The internal knowing of mankind is unlimited. The external expression of compassion and love is boundless. Let us move on to the next step of creation.

It is a time of realigning our thoughts and concepts of self in a way that produces harmony not only in our lives but in the lives of those around us. It is a time to reveal that we are not only capable of change but that we can do so with an understanding that we are part of nature's plan. A plan that calls for us to be aware of our commonality and not our differences.

What Do You Know about Light?

I suggest you write on a piece of paper or on a computer a list of what you know about light. Most of us in this day and age take light and its benefits for granted until we are not able to access it. This exercise is to awaken our memories based on current scientific knowledge. See appendix B for a summary of our present knowledge of light.

After listing what you know about light, put the paper aside and continue reading. I ask that you have an open mind to what you are about to read by being present, observing your actions, and detaching yourself as best as you can from judgment.

Our current perception of light is based on what we see and what science tells us. Light is much more than we accept in our current state of consciousness. We have been able to advance as a species because of light. Finding fire provided ancient man with warmth and protection. If you look at some of the ancient cave paintings, you can see it also gave them an ability to express their creativity. Now we use light in a variety of ways that allow our civilization to function. I am going to take the miracle of light in a different direction.

How do you define light? By the energy of your awareness to create something that embodies all of the world you inhabit. In other words, it is the energy of inclusion. The energy enables all and not a few. This is the time of the light of knowledge. It is the emergence of a creative call to all to better themselves through the betterment of others. The light works through the use of heartfelt intent. Awakening to that energy and level of awareness takes constant effort.

Moving to that which is apparent in the now requires awareness. The light that is embedded in darkness requires the understanding that one creates separation through darkness. The void of space appears as darkness. Lack of knowledge leads one to the same belief or conclusion. One does not realize that the lack of knowledge accepts that which is currently apparent. Light in the form of knowledge allows one to see that which is not obvious. Acceptance of life's current dynamic does not yield the potential that exists. Acceptance of a greater truth allows for the possibilities of future endeavors to be experienced in a higher level of awareness. No longer held by preconceived ideals, mankind becomes a dynamic force in the field of conscious evolution. It is the future manifested in the true realm of light.

Letting go of the past is not easy, but it is easier than you think. A way to release past practices of being require a willingness to learn more about light and its dynamics. The knowledge of light is based on your reference point—your conscious awareness of light. This is the ideal time to release information about the light quotient that is available to consciousness as it pertains to the lifecycle one leads. Light is the formation of creation. Light is the beginning of awareness, and light is the end of what is perceived as the current state of awareness and existence.

One exists in light to create. One exists in the continuum of light to be part of creation. The loss of conscious awareness of light is part of the drama existing in duality. Light is a fixture of existence. The lack of one's awareness of light does not change a person's place in existence. It changes his or her perception and experience of existence. One does not leave the realm of awareness without the use of light. One does not dwell in the realm of awareness without light as a guide. The only difference that is seen and experienced is how one chooses the path he or she journeys on. Each choice allows for light. How to become aware of and utilize this essential aspect of creation is up to the individual life and his or her choice within the realm of creation and desire to evolve.

No matter the life that is being lived, one does not separate from the light within. What takes the place of light is not what you think. The thought of darkness is an illusion. The intensity of darkness creates fear. The realm of awareness allows for the interpretation of the separation of light and dark. That is duality. That is a lack of knowledge and understanding. One does what one does for the experience of duality in form. The treasure of experience is lost when the focus becomes unbalanced, when light and dark are not an exchange of opposites but a dwelling place for the stagnation of beliefs in life's limitations. The opposite of attraction is reconciliation. When people create with limits as their point of awareness, their focus is not on cause and effect; it is on an excuse that justifies their experience.

The following is just a peek into what light truly is.

Light Is

- A generator of energy from the source of unlimited supply
- The opening in the dawn of a new creation
- The way to perceive what is hidden from consciousness
- The face of a new concept of creation
- The flow of an intention to create in a wave of unlimited potential
- The magic of life-giving resources in the form of energy and vibration
- One form of creation that man does not cherish
- The threefold application of existence in a natural state of creation
- A form of knowledge that is embedded in the landscape of one's mind
- Generated by complex fusion of particles that are drawn together by intent
- Sacred when understood as one of the building blocks of life
- The word of the divine in manifest form (refer to Genesis for clarity)
- A way to perceive the world from a higher point of conscious awareness
- The term in this material that leads to a greater understanding of man's role in a future context
- Divine knowledge residing in a form that is not easily understood when holding on to third-dimensional concepts

- The flame of sacred knowledge embedded in an intelligence that seeks receptivity
- The starlight of distant stars that originates in our hearts
- The sanctuary of our hearts that illuminates the workings of our eternal spark
- The beginning of the day when the light of knowledge meets the fallacy of our beliefs in separation and isolation
- Light divine from the Source of our creation

We are scared beings wrapped in the cloth of a material body. The reason for this experience is not hidden. It is just not easily accessed when the form and content are in a battle for supremacy. The workings of light as a form of acceptance greet the mind and heart in a way of illuminated thoughts. That which is to be is before the consciousness of man now. Light is being introduced so that we can realize it is not just something out there, something we are detached from. It is the opposite. The light of transition allows us to move forward with greater clarity.

What is clarity when described in the way of transition? Clarity is the awareness to proceed with knowledge and insight. Clarity is the wave of neutrality that provides for broader vision. It is the absence of illusion, and it is a gift. How can we describe clarity without including it as a gift? We cannot. The gift of sight or insight allows for a form of transition through harmony that is not available to the average person who holds the belief that what one sees is all there is.

Now, at this time, the light embedded in the realm of conscious thought is expanding. This expansion can create currents of opposing polarities. This means that too much energy in the form of light waves can have opposing effects that make for an unsettling experience. It can bring about the opposite of what one's expectations are in relationships, business transactions, and planned events. This form of experience is not necessarily harmonious and requires a foundation of belief, courage, and adaptability from those impacted.

The following are some clues or suggestions on how to handle the future as events unfold.

1) Take time to realize that the situation you find yourself in is an opportunity to let go of thoughts or possessions that no longer serve your growth as a person.

2) Take a moment to realize that you are a gift of life. This gift is one of creative expression. Ask for your inner voice to realize the strength you possess to move forward from the moment of your challenges.

3) Know from your heart and mind that each challenge is a way for you to proceed in life. Have faith that your journey is to be taken one step at a time. Place your faith in a greater Source (whatever form or concept of deity or energy you choose).

4) See your heart and mind in a straight line, and create a connection between the two. You can visualize a bridge, tube, or line. If visualization is difficult, feel a connection starting at the heart and moving up to the mind. Hold this visualization or feeling as you breathe in white light. Allow yourself to harmonize your breathing, and relax as best as you can. See a flame growing in your heart. Release the flame from your heart, and ask to receive the light of transition in a way that is more harmonious. State your willingness to receive the light, and accept it as done. Say an affirmation, such as "I AM the light of a new dawn that awakens me to a greater truth" or "I AM the light that flows now. My oneness is absolute. I AM."

5) Realize that the path you are on is receiving the light from a great Source. Allow the flow of light to be received with an open heart. Make sure it is light you are receiving, not the discordant thoughts and emotions of others. Meditation to understand the difference is greatly encouraged.

What one thing can you do in the midst of an unsettling event? The answer is personal. It is dependent on your current state of consciousness and your knowledge of who you are. Where are you strong, and where are you weak? What, if any, is your belief in the higher realms of spirit? Have you meditated in the past, or do you in the present, and how often do you pray? Each of these is an excuse, not the answer to the question, for you see, the divine in you sees no difference. One is not better than the other. As a matter of fact, the most unlikely of us may rise to the occasion better than the smartest and strongest or those seen as superior. The answer is to bring all of your attention to your heart and realize that you, in this moment, can let go of pain, suffering, and loss by allowing the Source of creation to be your guide. This may seem rather simplistic when all around is in disarray, but the Source is ever present and available to those who surrender their focus on Earth's experience to a higher form of divine guidance. I am reminded of a story about a group of nuns who prayed during the bombing of a Chinese city. Their prayer was to Quan Yin, the goddess of mercy and compassion. They prayed repeatedly through the bombing, repeating the same prayer over and over again. Eventually, the bombing stopped, and when they emerged from their building, they found that it was the only one left standing. All around them, they saw complete destruction and devastation.

The step of letting go is a big one due to the acceptance of the ego as personality and the embodiment of life and its role in your experience. This is not to confuse you from life itself. You are the consciousness of your awareness in life's drama. The role of the ego is protection. The confusion lies in who the ego is protecting and why. The whole drama of ego versus spirit is not that confusing when one realizes that spirit is forever, and the ego is an actor that has been consumed by its role in the third-dimensional drama. Each script is unique and requires full investment in the role. Though there are many parts to play, the ego thinks it is in charge. That is the beginning of a lost template of creation. The ego is the master of what, if it is not in charge of the script of your life? The answer for you is that you are an expression of divine sonship. The way to this realization is by realizing you are much more than your ego and have come here at this time for a greater purpose. Those who realize this truth are more willing to cope with events that are unsettling.

At this time, the answer to the present moment and present state of affairs is to seek balance. This is not just a challenge; it is the way forward for mankind and the planet. The winds of change are the order of the days, weeks, months, and years ahead. The nature of things now is in an accelerated form. This leads to many seeming obstacles and extremes. The way of the heart is a way of understanding that we can only control our reactions to life and the nature of things as they present themselves. Now more than ever, harmony is not just a goal; it is *the* goal. The way to achieve harmony is to change the focus on judgment of others and yourself. The light of a new day requires awareness and intent—awareness of self, as a form of expression and intent, not to play a part in a reactive mode but in a way, that brings harmony to yourself and others.

At this time, there is an opportunity to learn more than seems possible. There is a chance to awaken to a stream of consciousness embedded in the cycles of nature. This will bring revelations of thoughts and concepts that will propel mankind forward. The issue will be usage. It will require a state of awareness that seeks continually to use this form of advanced thinking in a way that benefits mankind. The enrichment of a few is not what these revelations are about. They require compassion, charity, and faith in a greater vision. Mankind has a test: wake up now, or sleep in ignorance for a span of time that is unavailable to this writer. This is not a doomsday scenario, for you see, mankind has been in this age of ignorance and darkness for a long time. Now is the time to wake up in the light. It shines for all to see.

Light is now the guide of this study to be revealed. The way mankind chooses is a matter of free will. It is a choice of direction. The patterns of reality that man has chosen are based on the concept that light is a vehicle of life in relation to daylight versus night. The sun is a generator of life, and the cycles of the seasons are governed by Earth in relation to the sun. In effect, the sun is a life giver, and without the sun, all would perish. The consciousness that created this equation is the same consciousness that believes in many forms of identity within the human race. It is the consciousness that tolerates pain, suffering, and destruction as a form of life. Now realize this: mankind is not an experiment in the eyes of creation. Mankind is an adaption of life in the evolution of creation. This means mankind has a place in the universe. His status is a matter for all of creation. *Intelligence* is just another word for status. When you raise your intelligence, you raise your status. What does this have to do with light?

Everything! Light is the basis for the evolution of man. Light is the connection between the race of man and the Creator of man. Light is a binding of the particles of life in a form that is sacred. The light that dwells within is sacred. The term *sacred* is the identification of something special, something out of the ordinary. The sacred in life is the beginning of a form of consciousness that does not rest in the image of man as it is currently conceived. Now is the moment of reflection. How willing are you to believe that you are sacred? Let me repeat that: How willing are you to believe that you are sacred?

Here is the clue. In the moment of your awakening to life, you were granted the blessing of breath. Does that mean that all of mankind has the ability to breathe when born? The answer is obviously no. There are those who, for whatever reason, are born with multiple challenges. The cause of their challenges is beyond the present scope of this material. I can only hint at what life's lessons are all about. What is important is that most of mankind is gifted with the blessings of breath. All of mankind is gifted with the spark of life that comes from the creative. The two gifts combine to create something known as humanity, the form and content of which are sacred. The spark of life dwells in all of humanity as an aspect of creation. The Source of our creation dwells within our spark or essence. The divide between the Source and the spark is due to our forgetfulness and acceptance of illusion, based in our core beliefs.

The moment of forgetfulness is not a constant for all who incarnate into physical form. This is due to the level of completion accomplished by the soul and the soul family that is present. The term *present* does not translate in human terms but is the progression of the states of expression that have been achieved. Forgetfulness is not only a lack of awareness but also a release of responsibility that does not burden the soul entering into third-dimensional reality. The saying "Ignorance is bliss" is partially correct in that one's life stream may be dedicated to achieving one task in this incarnation, and having memory may be too much of a burden to carry through the current lifetime.

There is another stream of thought that our forgetfulness is manipulated in some way—that we are in a stream or cycle of endless incarnations due to forces that are not in alignment with what is our highest good. This line of thinking and belief is all part of the myriad of scenarios that lead one on the path of duality. The true nature of what exists has many levels of reality based on one's beliefs. Our focus is on the light and dynamic of change leading us to a higher state of consciousness.

Our acceptance of illusion as part of existence in the third-dimension is part of the veils that conceal our true essence. Illusion is our willingness to be deceived by the beliefs that hold us in the state of consciousness that we accept as real.

The focus of memory is a key to the past and an opportunity for the future. What we know and what we learn are part of our path of evolution. The moment now is to focus on the light that shines within us and to bring about harmony, unity, and an individual and collective creation based on love and truth.

What Comes Next?

How fortunate that mankind dwells in a system of change that accommodates the transition of man from one vibratory realm of creation to another. How fortunate that the structure of reality is based on the finite and the infinite. How fortunate that the vehicles of change can grasp the meaning of life in the forms they currently possess. How is it that mankind dwells in isolation of his concepts of self when there are so many opportunities to be present with the truth of life? How does the current moment seem like just something that flitters by in an instant? It's like a breeze that flows by without anyone noticing or a breath taken without conscious thought.

The time of meaningful dialogue is at hand. The way of mankind today and the way of mankind tomorrow will be different in many ways. The first part of this material is about a happening. The second part of this material is to give you something to think about. The third part of this material is a way forward, and the fourth part of this material is destiny as a vision, a vision with meaning and a message. To wake now is not easy. To wake later is an issue to be recorded within one's higher nature. The form and content of life are to be expressed in accordance with the laws embedded in creation. How that takes place is the way of tomorrow brought forward to today.

Quietly, now we move from disorganization to a path of harmony. The harmonic expression of one's world is his or her journey demonstrated. The flow of one's vibration is like a wind in the realms of celestial space. When one speaks anger, his or her words ripple through the known universe. When one despairs, the form that the frequency takes of his or her emotion is recorded on the template of man. When one dwells in sorrow and regret, the universe of expression recognizes the disharmony of his or her experience. Mankind does not dwell alone. Mankind is part of a greater whole. Some have defined this as a hologram, where one part reflects and incorporates all. There is more to this than realized. A hologram is seen as an image, not as a continuous motion of intelligence and manifestation. The time for each of us to realize that we are part of an ongoing flow of conscious participation in something dynamic is the present moment. I know that this is not currently a realization that we can understand. This is due to the nature of the system of expression that we abide in. As seen from the planetary logos, we dwell in something that I will describe simply as a closed system. This means that from a universal standpoint, we have the opportunity to experience and grow in the confines of the space dedicated to the earthly experience. The time of arrival of a new template of existence is at hand. The meaning of what comes next is a conscious participation in growth and expansion. This may seem meaningless to some, but I can assure you these are not idle words.

Some will step forward on their paths of creation, and others will choose other directions. The road is open to all seekers. The path of creation is a blessing. Make of it what you will. You see, there is more than one way to achieve the goals of creation. We choose nonjudgment, but we advise discernment in all things. If your heart is hard, soften it. If your heart is soft, listen to it. If you believe that your heart is just to beat out its rhythm to satisfy your life, I suggest you take a moment to reconsider your views of the world you live in. If you speak to and through your heart, dwell more and learn in the cave of the heart. Bring forth the love you are by being. The essence of creation dwells within life. Our refinement allows nature to flow. This place of creation takes your involvement. It takes your conscious awareness. The road is through the heart, and the heart knows the way.

Release the concept of confinement that now dwells as human form. An intent of great significance is "I AM released from my prior commitment to the limits I have accepted as mine." See in the new sunrise an opportunity to change. The how of change is a broad subject, and it is dynamic if you will allow it to be. There is no one method for you to change your concepts of self. Because there is diversity, there is a wide selection to choose from when it comes to your personal growth. That said, I have dedicated this section to the process I feel works with the energy and direction of this material. It may not be the way that is your way. As I have said, there are many paths, but there is only one journey. Select the path that fills your heart with joy and your mind with wisdom. When done with love and openness, it is a blessing.

The title of this book is *The Emergence, A Time of Accelerated Change*. The following is a list of actions or ingredients you can use to adapt to what is taking place now and in the future.

Twelve Ingredients of Change
through the Emergence

1. Learn to be present.
2. Declare that you are worthy of the gift of life.
3. Listen to the inner words that create your reality.
4. Realize that there are no mistakes you cannot grow from.
5. The realm of life seeks your participation.
6. To learn something new requires an open mind.
7. What is so good or important that you are not willing to release it? (I am not talking about loved ones.)
8. See your thoughts as the foundation of your relationship to the world and self.
9. Realize you create your world continually. What is your motivation?
10. Make life more enjoyable by seeing what can be, not what can't be.
11. When you don't do something, realize that you have just done something.
12. The greatest restricting agents are fear, doubt, and guilt. What is the value of faith, trust, and gratitude?

The following is an explanation of the twelve ingredients of change through the Emergence.

1. Learn to be present.

Here and now are the greatest vehicle and opportunity to change. You are at the stoplight of life. The way forward is based on all your prior beliefs and concepts of life and how you exist in the earthly realm. Make up your mind to be present. By being present, you can make conscious decisions about how you react to life. You can see and become aware of your judgments. It is of value to realize that when you judge another, you are also judging yourself. It might take a moment or two for you to realize the validity of these words.

To be present requires your active participation in life, not responding to stimuli in an autoreactive manner. It also requires that you stand back as an observer. This will take some practice and patience. If you meditate, you have some experience with this practice. Breathing and watching your breath are good exercises to start with if you have never done this before. If you take tai chi or yoga, you can practice being present during your exercises.

Being present allows you to observe your actions and reactions. You can interrupt certain actions that you feel are detrimental to you as you change. We have all been cut off by drivers in a hurry, and most of us act out in anger. This reaction can easily be replaced with a sense of calm when you decide to change your reaction. The role of a red light when you are in a hurry raises your blood pressure significantly. You can, if you choose, do some breathing exercises to fill in where anxiety once ruled.

2. Declare that you are worthy of the gift of life.

How many of us do not believe we are worthy of anything good or joyful in our lives? When you were young and in your formative stages, did someone tell you that you would not amount to anything? Did you live in a poor neighborhood where men, women, and children lived lives that just barely met necessities? I did. I lived in an area of Chicago where we were just able to cover the basics. Today many of these areas, not just in Chicago but also around the world, are much poorer because of the dynamics of the times. Were you raised with physical and emotional violence? Did someone say to you, "You are not worthy of love and respect"? The truth of life is that you are a gift. Let me repeat that: you are a gift! The fact that you are part of this world makes you a living expression of that which is: creation. You are a spark of divine essence. You do not have to take my word for it. Let's look at some things for you to consider. You take breaths at regular intervals. Most can see all around them. You have beliefs, thoughts, and feelings. If I asked you to touch your heart with your left or right hand, what would you feel? Most might feel a gentle sensation. If I asked you now to think of one word and to place that word in your heart, such as *faith,* I feel certain you would sense something like a gentle expansion. The flow of your blood is in alignment with the flow of the essence of the earth. Your magnetic resonance is in alignment with the earth. The magic spiral in your body flows in accordance with the tempo of time, space, and place. This description could go on for many more pages, but the truth is that you are here for a reason, and your presence is a gift. Take a moment to realize the importance of this message.

Judgment of any type is a misplaced use of energy. When it comes to judging yourself, there are two aspects of your world that makes your judgment fuzzy. The first is that you do not realize your full structure of being. Those with the gift of spiritual and psychic sight and wisdom say we have seven bodies; most of us are familiar with one. The second is that we are told in many ancient texts, religious documents, and verbal wisdom traditions that we have a soul. The ancient Egyptians called this the BA. How many of us are currently in contact with our soul? The importance of who we are is hidden. At the present time, I am not in possession of the reason. I can only go by my desire to share this information. That includes the fact that the world was created so that we as members of the race of man could evolve into the higher realms of expression. With that as our statement of reality, we are active participants, and thus, we have been given the gift of life.

3. Listen to the inner words that create your reality.

How defined is this statement? How clear is its nature of what takes place in your reality? The focus is a statement of fact. Your inner words are your thoughts and inner dialogue. There are certain refrains that you consciously or unconsciously utter to yourself daily. These thoughts hold you in position. They are your dynamic force to create your reality. The fact that you are not aware of their power is part of the slumber that mankind is coping with. The power of words can be illustrated by the statement attributed to God: God said, "Let there be Light." Think for a moment on this command. Think for a moment on the power associated with the words. You do not see yourself as God, but you were created in his image. The disconnect between the concept of power and the ability to think and speak is readily apparent when you use words that are harmful and limiting. The power of thought creates, and the nature of your thoughts creates your world.

The focus of the internal speech you have is not just the image you expect from life and its events; it is the nature of your energy as a being of creation. The focus of your thoughts is specific and without direction when you utter words without thinking. How can words be specific and without direction at the same time? Let us say, for example, you are speaking to someone about another person. You are making judgmental comments about the persons' size and lack of proper appearance. Your words come from a place of judgment and difference. They are specific in tone and nature. What you do not realize is that your words have power. They are impacting the person you are speaking to and the person you are talking about. In addition, you are impacting yourself. Whether you realize it or not, words have a vibration and force. They do not go far from their source. Remember the saying "You reap what you sow." What are the seeds you plant when your thoughts become your words?

The nature of your internal dialogue can be changed. The desire has to come from a place of sincerity. Too many say they want to improve and then do little to make it happen. There are reasons, and there are excuses. All of the reasons and excuses lie within your internal dialogue, within your belief of the power, or lack thereof, in life. I understand that there are circumstances in which, through physical or mental conditions, the die appears to be cast. I say unto you that the nature of creation is unlimited; it is infinite. The will of love and life is stronger than our ability to comprehend. The will of that which is among us cannot falter or fail.

4. Realize that there are no mistakes you cannot grow from.

All of mankind believes to one degree or another in judgment. The dialogue of the time is based on one person's success and another person's failure. It is based on judgment. Let us see judgment for what it truly is: judgment is the distance between truth and illusion. Judgment is based on facts or circumstances that one assumes are real, when in reality, things are not what they appear to be. What about murderers and terrorists who kill innocent people? Those facts are real, are they not? This is the drama of hatred versus love within the collective consciousness of man. This is where the opposite of what is taking place must have an alternate cause of action. A level of judgment is not what those situations call for. They call for a lack of judgment, a refrain from the game of opposites. The current level of consciousness accepts and expects that bad things will continue to happen as long as man pursues his current course of thoughts and beliefs based on existing norms. There is a time and place for the rebalancing of the dramas of

Earth. No amount of words can convey that the issue starts with what we find acceptable. The line of thinking of action and reaction is in our hands. We have to learn to grow from the mistakes we make and change the habit patterns that give rise to extreme responses.

The way to grow is through experience. The way to increase your consciousness is through the direct application of your creative self to learn, express, and be. What people learn is what they desire in life based on their thoughts and beliefs. There are some people who marry the same type of person that they believe they desire or are attracted to. After several marriages and divorces, they find the right person who provides them with the love and support they deserve. It took several attempts to find that they were attracting the wrong person into their life. This type of scenario is repeated at many levels before success comes from the foundation built on their prior mistakes. Thomas Edison made many mistakes before he developed several inventions that we rely on today. How many avenues are tried by entrepreneurs before they are successful? Failure is not the end of a journey; it is the opportunity to grow from the knowledge one has received. I have a saying on my desk that states, "What would you attempt to do if you knew you could not fail"?

The importance of doing is fundamental in change. The way of the now is to realize the focus of believing that there is no waste of effort when going through the learning and experiencing the process of life. Each step along the way has value when you realize that your purpose in life is to learn about your gifts and then use those gifts to benefit yourself through growth and through the contributions you make to the world around you.

5. The realm of life seeks your participation.

How often have you gone to a classroom, business meeting, church service, or public debate and chosen to sit in the back? How often in group settings have you had questions you did not ask for fear of being judged? We have been given our lives for a purpose. The only way to begin to realize that purpose fully is to engage actively in the process of life.

What do I mean by actively engaging in the process of life? The role you have chosen is yours. Some will hold the belief that no one or thing other than our Divine Source can alter that. The truth of existence is the level of latitude we have in creating our own destiny. My goal is to awaken you to that which is possible. Your participation in life is based on the path you have chosen. Some type-A personalities are highly active and appear successful. For the majority of people, outside winning a lottery, life has a pretty set routine. Your direction in life is accepted as part of your destiny. The rub comes in when things don't always work out as planned or when you are still searching for that lightbulb to go off to give your journey meaning. Here is the moment you have been waiting for. You are doing exactly what you and others expect you to do. I am not being fatalistic when I make that statement. The combination of life choices, the central theme of your beliefs, and the expectations you have of life have fulfilled your present state of being. The time of the Emergence calls for a different set of parameters. This is a time to realize that the accepted norms are being replaced by energies that require your participation not in isolation or separation but as part of a conscious awareness that you are capable of achieving. It is far more than you think.

The flow of life is vibrant when the life force is balanced and engaged. The process of life follows the plan of nature. When we engage our abilities, we become more, not less, of a force within nature. Watch a stream as it flows normally along its predetermined path. Watch a stream when its source has been devoid of rain or snow. Then watch as a stream becomes a torrent when there is an abundance of rain or snow. The extremes are usually more noticeable when the source is lacking or in excess. The idea of participating in life is to find a balance, to find the right source. This is a life lesson. Seek what is available through your heart's desire. I am not talking about possessions or longings. I am talking about the truth within that seeks your awareness.

6. To learn something new requires an open mind.

There is a step-by-step progression to learning. This progression is based on the openness of one's willingness to learn. This may seem obvious, but you have to recognize the fact that some people are resistant to learning anything. The judgment is "They are set in their ways." The truth is that learning is a lifelong process. Each day, something comes our way that we accept as fact. Each day, there is a new revelation about something. It can be new technology or a new event that shapes our world. This openness is based on our willingness to accept what is given from external sources. The issue comes when we are asked to change habits or beliefs. If we have a belief about something, it might take something dramatic to change it. If we have a recurring habit, such as smoking, drinking, or doing drugs, changing the habit is difficult without a form of intervention, be it physical, mental, emotional, or spiritual. The stimulus for change is usually an extreme of some sort.

The focus of change is not the vehicle we normally chose. It is usually something that gets our attention and will not let go. Giving up a habit or belief requires a willingness to listen and an openness to consider what is being presented. The focus of our subject is opening the mind to realize that there are other sources of information, knowledge, and tools that can assist you in changing the nature of your perception of yourself and the universe.

The format of changing the view one has of the world requires a different set of dynamics. When one receives knowledge that is counter to his or her accepted beliefs, the first reaction is doubt or refusal to accept what is being given. It's important to have a willingness to explore the possibility that what is being given has validity. This is a way change can take place. Change requires your willingness to let go of existing beliefs so that you can access greater concepts of reality. Relying on the current standards of reality is fixing your position so that there is a greater chance you will not hear or be willing to receive the message. Now is an opportunity to alter prior concepts of life and its creations.

7. What is so good or important that you are not willing to release it?

The time that it takes to release any aspect of life that no longer serves your higher good is proportionate to your willingness to change. The stuff of a lifetime is like a substance that is attractive to you and those around you. We are the composition of the life we have chosen to live. Now there is a realization that habits and concepts of self have a property that in effect sticks to us based on the frequency of the patterns of reality each of us demonstrate. There is a magnetic quality to who and what we are. We attract the substance of life based on the path we have chosen. If we are attracted to things and situations based on our inner dynamic and in turn attract them based on our beliefs and thoughts, how do we release things, ideas, and beliefs that no longer serve and have not served our higher good?

Release is the letting go of things. This requires some thought. Don't make a home for them. If there is no room for them, then they have to go somewhere. It is your role to release what restricts or limits your ability to rise to the level of your true nature. Herein is the focus. The truth is, all beliefs and thoughts are transitory. They are not truly yours, but you choose to see them as yours. They are energy that is not stagnant; they are in a vibration that you must reach down to receive. This is part of the solution. What is so enticing about beliefs in separation, limitation, and judgment that you are willing to lower your vibration for?

The answer is conditioning. We have been conditioned to accept the less in life. Why is this an accepted way of life? The rhythm of the universe calls for a wide spectrum to that which is creation. The flow of knowledge that we accept as real is in a narrow range of our abilities to comprehend higher forms of intelligence. Because of our accepted levels of consciousness, we choose through third-dimensional thinking what appears as reality. This allows us the ability to accept lower and slower forms of what appears as logic and reason. This is not judgment; it is the reason we accept current forms of life as our expressions of self. The timeline for us to access higher vibrations and, thus, break the bonds of restrictive thought and beliefs is at hand.

8. See your thoughts as the foundation of your relationship to the world and self.

The way of now chooses the path that leads to a greater understanding of self. What is self, and how do we identify with it? One way of looking at the greater aspect of self is through third-dimensional lenses as an embodiment of soul and spirit. The thing that makes this challenging is the lack of knowledge and direct experience related to both aspects of creation. Man dwells in human form and identifies more with personality and ego than soul and spirit. This disconnect leads to the illusion that mankind is here to suffer and experience pain. What one believes is nearly certain to happen one way or another. The lack of understanding of the true nature of man has led to the states of consciousness that now seem to rule the landscape of Earth. In some ancient circles, this condition was described as being asleep, and in others, it was deemed the lack of remembering. The foundation of man is not only obscured from view; it is almost completely forgotten.

New children are being born now into the condition of man. These children will look at and are looking at reality with a more questioning approach. Their innocent request for truth and unity is a call to all humanity to realize that transition from old concepts to what is evolving requires our conscious participation. All along, the foundation you are is the truth in motion. You are the equivalent of a moving tapestry, and the strokes of your actions are reflected on the canvas of life. Open yourself to realize that you are a projection of some aspect of creation that is evolving. Once you lend yourself to this vision, you will pay more attention to life and to living.

The foundation of life as it is currently being lived is accepted for that which is. This acceptance is in effect a structure of consciousness that perceives reality as fixed. It is accepted as is. Now is a good time to realize a greater truth of reality. Your foundation requires a greater awareness. What was taken for granted as reality has more than a few issues. These issues include the disconnect of mankind from one another; the true nature of man's right and ability to create in harmony with the universe; and the determination that the Source has many faces and that the only life in the universe is material in form.

9. Realize you create your world continually. What is your motivation?

What is the foundation of your life? What are your beliefs? Can you list them, and if you do list them, are you comfortable with what you see? If you choose not to list them, why not? Is there something within your beliefs that you are reluctant to see or experience?

I have asked quite a few questions. Only you have the answers, because they are your beliefs. I do not judge what your motivation is in life, because I have not walked the path of your life and had your life experiences. I have stated many times through this material that you are responsible for your creations and life experiences based on your life lessons, beliefs, thoughts, and actions. I hope to convey that you are a perpetual-motion machine. You may rest as a form of regeneration, but even then, you are creating the events of your life. You can point out accidents happen to innocent people. Illness takes some people before they have lived full lives. A random act of terrorism might injure and kill innocent people. We read and see extreme levels of intolerance currently being demonstrated. How can we say we are responsible for our experiences? Because it comes from a greater vision of life. We do not know the reasons bad things happen to good people. We do not know if the reason is karma, the lessons of reincarnation, the attraction of negative events based on fear, or false beliefs. We cannot, nor will we, judge another's motive for life, but the life you lead is the life your energy in creation is attracted to.

The formula for life is simple: take one-part love, add a drop of energy and a dash of spirit, and mix gently with courage. It takes courage to lead the life that is of the mind that we are all one—one people, one spirit, one life. All around us we see just the opposite. We see destruction, distrust, and disease. The motivation you have dictates your journey. I hope and pray that the information and knowledge I am sharing will open your eyes a little wider to allow a ray of light to enter your concept of self, thus leading you on a quest for more knowledge and wisdom.

10. Make life more enjoyable by seeing what can be, not what can't be.

This old saying is based on optimism or pessimism: "Do you see the glass as half full or half empty?" Each of you is of the same glass. Your answer is totally based on your state of mind and how you view the world. That is what we are told. What we're not told to consider is why the same glass looks different to a variety of people. There is a closed view of one's world, and there is an open view. The mind is like a door that opens and closes to possibilities. This may be viewed as optimism and pessimism, or it can be based on one's knowledge and expectation of life. What if you were never taught through your parents' modeling, peer modeling, and accepted beliefs that you were capable of looking for options in life? What if the potential of any situation was never really understood for what it was? Some will say that options and possibilities are all around us. The quandary is this: How do you see them when you have never been taught where to look? Before we judge too harshly, how many of us have been in situations or relationships where we thought there was no way out? How many of us are in this situation or predicament right now?

There are those who see the only way out of their current situation is to end their life. To terminate their suffering. What if someone had shown them a different way out, would they still be alive today. I don't know the answer to that question because of the variations of our energy patterns and our life lessons. The point that I am trying to make is there are usually options if you are willing or know where to look. The options of life are twofold: to live and to die in physical form. The Infinite Mind of Creation states that life is a series of steps that can lead you to a place where *potential* is not just a word for life coaches and successful people. Potential is the activation of your indwelling spirit to express the creativity of your gifts. Potential is the wellspring of innovation that comes forth when welcomed with the spirit of your belief in life and what life holds.

We have to factor in the presence of the ego in our current state of existence. It is the action of the ego that seeks renewal through things. When one abides with the ego as a main form of expression there is a loss of the true purpose of being. The ego is meant to protect and to satisfy the imagined needs of what is identified as the personality. When we allow the life stream we are to come forth the image we have of our self changes. We begin to realize that we are more than our current configuration of consciousness allows us to be.

The Mind of Creation is infinite because we are its embodiment. The Mind of Creation is the birthplace of ideas, and if you contemplate that thought, you realize we are an idea. We are a thought in the mind of our Creator, a thought that has manifested in the realm of the third dimension. Some might say they can't believe that. How can we be an idea in the mind of our Creator? The idea that we are the creation of an omnipotent aspect of All There Is is not unrealistic when we remove the egocentric concept of self and realize the unity of life and that the resulting diversity is all part of creation's plan.

The realm of the possible is ready and able to facilitate your vision. One must realize that there is a difference between fantasy and vision. One has been given certain gifts in life. Use those gifts, expand your knowledge, and look for opportunities where you can prove to yourself and others that a clear outlook on life includes faith, trust, and joy. Henry Ford is quoted as saying, "If you say you can't do something, then you can't." I say if you expect the world to be better than it appears, hold to that vision, and create the intention to make it so. You are an aspect of creation that cannot be denied if you refrain from negating your capabilities.

11. When you don't do something, realize that you have just done something.

The call of your natural self seeks expression. When you were a child, you would get attention by crying. That is a form of expression. The act of expression is all around you. When flowers bloom, they are expressing their true nature. The fall of one's life is the expression of life as we age. The accomplishment of any endeavor is the result of your expression to be more than you were yesterday. When you share an experience with friends or family, it is an expression of your desire to experience life. The act of expression in the hands of a lumberjack is to bring down a tree. We are fully engaged in most activities that bring us joy, even those we take for granted. There are moments, however, when we choose not to act. We decide, *No, I am not doing that chore today.* With every decision not to act or participate in life, we have created an action. Your expression of your creativity is put on hold. What takes place is the opposite of the flow of energy and life force. It is a stoppage. When enough of these nonevents take place for whatever reason, the energy builds and, in many cases, becomes stagnant or blocked. This can lead to a variety of issues related to one's life force.

The direction of your life turns on your daily decisions. I know based on my age that if I decide not to or cannot exercise for any reason for more than two days in a row, I become stiff and lethargic. If more time passes without my exercising, it becomes harder and harder for me to get back into some type of physical activity. You can say the same thing about a variety of other activities. The point here is that not doing is doing something that is contrary to your inner nature. I know people will say, "I cannot exercise," or "I cannot go for long walks or play with my grandchildren," because of a variety of reasons. I fully believe that where there is a will, there is a way. You may not be able to do the things you used to do or do them the way you would choose to, but there are ways nonetheless that you can still accomplish some things. The Wounded Warrior Program demonstrates what wounded servicemen and servicewomen can accomplish when the spirit of their internal drive and will is activated. I hope you can find within yourself ways to accomplish other aspects of creation in your life. We are all here for a purpose. Let that purpose be your reason for being.

Going through life without a seeming purpose is the result of the world we have chosen to experience. Within each of us is a purpose. The role we choose has clues to our passage through the challenges of life. For some, their purpose seems well defined. For some, it comes later in life through events that are miraculous in nature. For some, it is a spiritual calling. For others, the path to their purpose is not that clear. The time for each one to find greater clarity in life is at hand. Inaction as an expression of life is becoming more challenging because the energy we are experiencing is more intense now than in the past. Take each moment as a sign that life is here for you to find and express not only your gifts but also your potential.

12. The greatest restricting agents are fear, doubt, and guilt. What is the value of faith, trust, and gratitude?

We come now through a portal. The entrance is dark and moist, but we can see light and hear sounds that we cannot identify. We were safe in the womb, allowed to grow with warmth and hear only a sound that gave us comfort: the beat of a mother's heart. Suddenly, we know something has happened to change all that. The light and new sounds are startling. We have movement, and something is holding us. Then there is pain, and we let out something that frightens us even more. For most of us, this is our introduction to life in physical form. The result sets the stage for us to enter a life that is both bewildering and serene at the same time. A mother's touch and that familiar sound of the heartbeat are reassuring. This is a moment of reflection. It is also a moment of structure, the establishment of relationships, and bonding. This time will pass quickly, and all will change based on the circumstance of character and the life path of the parents.

As life evolves, so too does the introduction of knowledge. We learn what we can and can't do. One learns what to fear and what it is to make choices. One learns what is rewarded and what is not. Some learn they are different, and others learn the difference between abundance and lack. They learn fear and survival. Some learn that what a person says is not in accord with his or her actions. Others learn that their actions lead to penalties that change the course of their lives. In short, for most of us, the world can be a place of fear, doubt, and guilt. I have chosen these three aspects of experience and expression because they are the most restrictive when it comes to their impact on the structure of our ability to evolve. I could write a book or two on these three subjects, but that is not the focus of this work.

The active concepts of fear, doubt and guilt are an obstruction on our road to the fullness of life. The veil these aspects of life create are in opposition to the wonders we can produce. We can reduce fear, eliminate doubt and nullify guilt through awareness and a sincere desire to realize that a greater knowledge exists within us, if we are willing to find it. Knowledge can be liberating when we seek the truth.

To cover every aspect of life's challenges would be impossible since most of us experience many of life's challenges as we go through the various stages of life. It seems that for every up, there is a down. We accept the reality that we are in a realm of seeming opposites. For many, there is faith in a brighter future. For others, there is no course of action other than to find a way to survive. The truth associated with the change that is taking place is that we are going to evolve. What path of life you take is up to you. It is your free will to choose the direction and destiny of your life. This is a moment when life changes, and we can choose to focus on the attributes of faith, trust, and gratitude.

Faith, Trust, and Gratitude

The course of life that is before us requires an expansion of consciousness and awareness. The term *mindfulness* is appropriate, as is the term *heartful*. I believe that the expressions of faith, trust, and gratitude are vital ingredients in our evolutionary process.

Faith comes from our heart. There is an exercise I will share that reveals a higher frequency of the use of faith. Please see the end of this section.

Faith

Faith is the action in which you allow yourself the opportunity to share a vibration of direct thought with your higher aspect of creation. Life is the vehicle you have chosen to experience what it's like to be in third-dimensional form. This form of expression holds many challenges. When you turn your inner expectations over to a higher aspect of creation, the soul is allowed to expand. Your potential for a more cohesive set of experiences is set in motion. The challenge is to maintain your faith through opposing energies in the form of life experiences. The truth of your experience is tested because of events and relationships you have created through beliefs and thought-based energies from the past. Current events are based on past beliefs and expectations. Your stream of conscious and subconscious thoughts and beliefs manifests when energies line up to allow for their manifestation.

Faith is the realm of the heart. Heart energy is little understood by most third-dimensional inhabitants. The energy of your heart is intelligent. It is not just a series of waves. It understands your greater truths. This means there is a connection within the heart to the realm of consciousness that is the basis for this material. The way is open to reveal its truths when you are open to receive it. The act of faith is not something to be dismissed without considering the alternatives.

Faith is an act of refined imagery. Faith is a position of openness and receptivity. One may be open to an event, such as a miracle, but it is your awareness that something related to your act of faith is actually taking place. Miracles happen all the time, but some seem so normal that the events are missed. Faith in the world around us is seen as a form of expansion. Allow the ingredients within the miracle of faith to manifest in your life.

Trust

The act of trust involves giving up preconceived notions of what is going to happen. Trust is the aspect of life that is described as letting go. You are trusting that something positive will take place. Trust can be described as letting down your guard (i.e., your preconceived expectations) so that events will come to something you see as positive.

Whereas faith comes from the heart, trust appears to be more of a mental activity. The focus of trust is on outcomes. Trust is related to your sense that actions or events will be an improvement over today. Something you set in motion or asked others to set in motion will give you a greater sense of freedom.

Trust is a fountain with two faces. Trust is usually placed in a person or situation. The aspect of trust that I am focused on is the one that is based in truth. Discernment is a required aspect of trust. One does not give trust lightly. It is a form of deception when dealing with people or situations that are not based in integrity. This is where the mind and heart can work together to create an environment for growth of experience and growth of expression. The concept of integrity in this material seems to indicate a form of integration of beliefs in a realm of higher states of awareness.

Gratitude

Gratitude is the realization that what one has is a gift. It is the opening of the door to allow greater expressions of life to enter. The mind of man sees material objects as possessions. The right to own anything is considered a normal aspect of life. There is not a realization that most things are a form of energy. Their ownership is a state of mind. It is not the true nature of creation. Most things appear and disappear based on the form of our creative expression. A family in Ohio was caught in a tornado. The wind hit so fast that they were barely able to seek the safety of their basement. When they emerged unhurt, their home and possessions were completely destroyed. Grief and fear overwhelmed them. The mother sought to comfort her children. She said to them, "They are only possessions. We have one another, and we can build again." This is gratitude for life and an expression of a greater truth. We came to life to learn and grow. When we leave physical form, we take nothing with us but memories, knowledge, and a realization that we are spirit first.

Gratitude is the great equalizer. Being grateful is an act of attrition. It is a realization that what one possesses has been created for him or her for a purpose. Most do not take time to realize there is a purpose to what surrounds them. The gift of vibrant health is there for them to accomplish the tasks of life—not with half an effort but with the full intent of their hearts' desire. The abundance of money in a person's life is meant not to be hoarded or used for selfish means but to be used for the good of the heart's directed expression. The lack of anything is also a gift, as hard as that seems to a person who is feeling the pain and discomfort of lack. The use of limitation is a lesson of life to learn and grow from. The law of manifestation does not pick and choose who has abundance and who has lack. The choice is in each one of us to express our potential. This is the way of the now: to learn and to realize that we are not finite but infinite. Gratitude, when it comes from a place of awareness, is like a magnet to a higher perception of life. We can begin to break the chains of darkness that we have used to create the insufficiencies of life.

Gratitude is a blending of what is apparent and what is not apparent. The thought that one is grateful for a child with a terminal disease appears on the surface to be contradictory. When one listens to the reason for the gratitude, you have an inkling as to what holds the love of life. The purpose of gratitude is to share with the universe a consciousness that is uplifted by thought, reason, and awareness. A life lived in gratitude is a life that dwells in the blessing of universal creation. Life is the love of receptivity when born in the consciousness of what creation truly means.

The realm of life is filled with opportunities. The expression of what and who we are is in alignment with our beliefs. How do we change when change is called for? How do we move past the barrier of the unknown aspects of life? When seen from an elevated point of observation, our lives seem to have continuity. There is what appears as a steady progression of time and events. Yes, there are disruption and unforeseen events that alter that progression. That is when change seems to be forced upon us. We can choose doubt, fear, and sometimes guilt, or we can choose a higher form of receptivity and expression. The following is a way to direct our energies upward, if you will.

An Exercise in Faith, Trust, and Gratitude

The way to use the heart, mind, and soul connection is to take a deep breath in a location that is quiet. If you have a place of meditation and contemplation, that is excellent. I ask that you gently enter into a calm state.

Tell your mind that you are safe. As you inhale, begin to focus on your heart. After several gentle breaths, say, "I AM light. Not just ordinary light but white opalescent light."

Feel, if you can, white light in and around you.

As you inhale, say, "I AM faith," and as you exhale, say, "I AM."

Sense faith as it moves through your consciousness. There is no need to rush.

As you inhale, say, "I AM trust," and as you exhale, say, "I AM."

Sense trust as it moves through your consciousness from your heart up to your mind. Take your time. The flow of consciousness will feel a sense of release.

As you inhale, say, "I AM gratitude," and as you exhale, say, "I AM."

Sense gratitude as it moves through your consciousness. Let your gratitude float freely as on the wings of a dove.

Be aware of the responses your senses are registering.

Take a deep breath and relax.

Let faith, trust, and gratitude be present in your life. Let the three expressions of a higher form of love take you to a place of greater understanding. You can repeat this exercise two or three times, whatever is most comfortable.

Another way of working with the three aspects of life—faith, trust, and gratitude—is to view them in the form of a triangle. In the prior exercise, they were treated as separate acts of conscious intent. You can create on a piece of paper or computer a triangle to use as a reminder or as a form of reinforcement.

When you have a moment, tell yourself to focus. Once you feel comfortable, say the following, and as you do, sense the feeling and impressions you are receiving:

Faith, Trust, and Gratitude

See faith at the top of the triangle. On the lower left, at the base, see trust, and on the lower right, see gratitude. As inhabitants of the third dimension, we've used the triangle as a teaching form, the way to insight and conveyance of knowledge. This is the work of wisdom that has proven to be an important vehicle for mankind's process based on historical events.

The present use of this triangle is to provide you a way to assist in your transition from self to a higher form of understanding. It is also a way to assist you in handling the events that are currently taking place in life. This is a way to facilitate growth. It is not the only way, for there are many paths. This is the one we are working with, and it appears to link to a greater understanding that follows this material.

The next level of this exercise is to think about what you are trusting, what you are grateful for, and where you are placing your faith. You can keep a journal or notes for yourself. I have found this seemingly straightforward exercise to be the foundation for something of great significance. I feel blessed that this exercise is not the end of the change within the Emergence; it is the continuation of an evolutionary process that takes mankind on an interesting and rewarding journey. Time is imaginary, but love is not.

When the time is right, there is a requirement to realign your thinking and concepts of self with the timing and rhythms of the moment. With that in mind, I have developed what I call a realignment declaration. This declaration is designed to assist in getting a greater understanding of certain thoughts and ideals that may not align with the changing times. This is not a blank check to feel that all of the ills of the world will dissipate with this declaration. It is one more step in a series of steps necessary to bring about a change in conscious awareness. Simply stated, you get out of it what you put into it.

The following realignment declaration can be done every morning as part of one's meditation or daily ritual before breakfast or exercise.

Realignment Declaration

Take a moment to focus on the love you are. Bring your focus to the center of your heart chakra. See the flame of a candle at the heart chakra, and say the following:

I am the sun[8] of the light that guides this day, this moment.

All that is no longer, holds the patterns of illusion that have been the basis for my earthly experience.

I am the light from the rising sun that illuminates my thoughts and ideals and reveals a greater truth.

That truth now aids me in releasing forevermore my sense and belief in lack and limitations of my ability to create in light.

I am the love of the divine; my perfection in the risen light is now revealed.

I am the light of the divine; my patterns of reality are now cleansed, and I move on to my true loving purpose in life.

---

[8] The word *sun* is not misspelled; it is used to assist you in seeing a new sunrise that provides greater clarity. It is also a moment to realize that you, like the sun, are a radiant aspect of life.

Let freedom come forth from divine light now.

May I choose wisely my path of perfection, my path of unlimited love.

May my freedom reveal greater clarity on my path of creation, in alignment with light, love, and truth.

I AM. Yes, I AM.

Third Wisdom Stratum

How often do you awake and bless the day?

How often do you bless the day by your actions, thoughts, and deeds?

How do you judge one's journey when you do not know his or her story?

Section 4

***

Destiny as a Vision

The field of absolute perfection is not a dream but a reality of conscious living. The way for mankind is set to achieve more, not less, than that which is defined by cosmic law. The term *life* is not just for the living in this time-space continuum. Existence is the manifestation of a plan of evolution and expansion. This means events are not happenstance. They do not and cannot happen arbitrarily and without cause. The light of understanding calls for the recognition that all things manifest and unmanifest are the product of the laws of creation. This reality is a result of a combination of events that created the foundation for this illusion to materialize. It is the focus of a million wants, a million desires, and a million lessons that have been interwoven to create a platform to grow into truth. The challenge has been to realize that what appears real is a phantom of reality. That which appears as blood and bone is a mixture of stuff from universal consciousness, which is a desire for knowledge, wisdom, and the realization that separate anything, when accepted as fact, is fantasy. The only dream that is real in this realm is one of unity—unity of heart, mind, and soul, not just of the *I* of man but the all of life.

What Is the Destiny of Mankind?

How do you answer what seems unanswerable? There are many options and possibilities, some good and some not so good. What is the destiny of the lives of many of Earth's bound souls? The answer has to come from a different spectrum of truth, from a place not of limitation and grief but of possibilities. Here is the vision that comes forth from that spectrum of reality that sees what can be.

This vision came to me at two different times. As I started to write the first time the vision came in what seemed at the time to be an endless stream of information. The second time just picked up where the first session ended. I have not made any changes to the vision I received nor am I aware of the timeline to bring this vision to fruition.

Mankind in the future knows that one land is not different from another. People know that the only difference in geographic location that is of importance is lifestyle. Mankind has learned the lesson of communication with one another. Individuals have realized that it is of prime importance to address one another with respect and dignity. The lessons of the past have shown that disagreements are a lack of understanding and tolerance for one another. The future is seen as an opportunity to create a harvest of plenty when ideas, concepts, and plans are made for the greater good of all.

The concept of unity is based on the realization that each and every spark of life is a gift. Differences are seen as diversity of creation, not as something to be judged. The role of one is made to assist the growth of the children. Love is not seen as a weakness or as the sole attribute of the heart. Love is seen as a strength of creative intention. Mankind has come to learn that the blending of heart and mind is the opportunity to create in harmony with the nature of the earth.

Each and every soul that comes into Earth's expression learns to release the discordant thoughts and feelings of past experiences. Nowhere does man drink or dine alone. The community of mankind has been expanding its understanding and utilization of the ways of unity of action. Creativity is like reaching for the stars. There are no limits. The food of the earth is grown with a sense of responsibility and eaten with the wonderment of a child at play.

The first letter that each child is taught is *l*, which stands for *light*, as in the brilliance of the suns both seen and unseen, the illumination of ideas and concepts in the world of a child's imagination, and the room filled with light that children create with their presence. Light is a way to open doors to the innocence of children's true nature. Adults are the vehicle of transmission, and as such, they will learn a new language: the language of light of responsibility to see and share with their children the concepts of the sacred nature of life. Each and every child is seen for what he or she truly is: the future of the world.

Earth is no longer seen as a convenient place to dwell. It is seen as a vehicle of the nature of things. Life is not used and then tossed aside. It is the second *l* taught to children and adults. Life is a vehicle to move through the lessons of existence. Life is not seen as the breath we now take for granted but is revered for its many properties. As such, we do our best to make air breathable for all living beings, including plants, animals, and humans. Factories and companies are using natural resources in ways that we have just begun to discover. Land is no longer owned. It is seen as a gift from nature, and it belongs to nature. This lack of ownership is not seen as a loss of wealth. Viewing land as a possession created strife in the past, but that view is no longer valued because of the realization that Earth is for all of its inhabitants. This transition of consciousness was not accomplished overnight. It took many decades and several phases to accomplish.

Values are not based on possessions or positions. Consumables are equally distributed because all on Earth are seen as an integral part of society and creation. This perspective takes a significant shift in consciousness. The creations of this time are valued based on their contribution to society. Improving what one has is not valued as we presently perceive value. Improving what is for the collective whole is valued. This possibility is seen now as a utopia or nonsense, but when we begin to realize our greater truths, we will understand that possessions can be a limiting factor in our personal and societal advancement.

That which is to be is like a light unto the heavens. Mankind will dwell in an atmosphere of greater understanding and knowledge. People will more fully understand and accept their roles in a universe of hierarchies. This new level of understanding will allow them the motivation to excel at the game of life. The relationship of man to nature will take on a new dimension, and mankind will produce the fruits of his endeavors with a new and greater understanding and awareness of cause and effect. Because the role of creating in harmony with the laws of nature will be better understood, mankind will endeavor to rectify the imbalances of the past. This will be done using the latest of technologies to identify where a lack of knowledge existed that gave rise to warfare, atrocities, and the improper use of power. Because of the extensive nature of this endeavor, mankind will work on the process for an extended period of time. How long this will take is not part of what is seen. Those who have a sense of unfinished business related to this endeavor will grow in their roles as members of a collective consciousness that pursues the rebalancing of earthly energies.

The spiritual pursuit of man will take different paths as new knowledge and wisdom are gained through a focus on achieving higher realms of thought and awareness. New sciences will evolve as mankind delves deeper into the many matrices of creation that are currently undiscovered or cannot be explained based on the current level of consciousness at this time. One of the sciences will deal with the humanistic nature of man, not from the level of mind but from the inner levels of the heart spectrum. Mankind will develop an understanding of harmonics in relation to the patterns of reality that are manifesting. The cloning of species will cease once man realizes the nature of spirit in all living things. The use of medicine that is prevalent today will be placed in museums as prehistoric. The body of the future will be better understood, as well as the reasons for disease. The use of light, color, and vibration will aid in cures, but the causes of the afflictions will be identified through more enlightened processes hidden from sight at this time.

Mankind will enter a new mode of transportation that uses waves of energy. These energies will be highly focused and restricted to just the movement of goods and human transport. Because these waves of energy can be disruptive to human activities, they will be used at regulated times and in predetermined areas. The movement of ideas and concepts of education will be broadcast on new and existing wavelengths but with much greater clarity and at faster speeds. The knowledge of today will be fully recorded and used as a platform to demonstrate how new ideas and beliefs are generated and made to manifest from the Infinite Mind of Creation.

Human study will be a process that everyone will participate in. The idea of limits will be seen as primitive by the standards of the time. Wars will have disappeared from the landscape of Earth, but the work of refining the energies and thought forms that created them will still be a challenge. The darker nature of man may have been identified, but the role of bringing harmony to one's nature is still ongoing. The lands where wars and famine have taken place have to be rebuilt to bring the earth back into balance. The role of finding and demonstrating balance at all levels of society is the ongoing work of mankind. Teachers will appear who will show that some of the old ways of mastery of self are still viable, but they will use a new way of communicating so that the messages are not shrouded in mystery or secrecy.

As the vision continues, mankind has a new sense of order. The rules of the nations have changed to accommodate the lack of boundaries. The ancient languages are still taught, but they are used more now as a stimulus for the capacity within the brain. Music and mathematics are used to stimulate and exercise the mind so that teachers can aid students in achieving greater levels of awareness and creativity. The language of the heart is taught from the earliest of grades. Actually, the term *grades* are no longer used because of the expansion of knowledge. The level of study that a child or adult takes in education is based strictly on his or her interest level, goals, and innate abilities. Each is seen as a genius, for no one else can duplicate what he or she can achieve. Here uniqueness is praised for its potential. A person is not judged for what he or she can't do but encouraged to do what is within.

The medical department of the city, town, or center is like the hub of a spoke. There are many specialties, but the focus of diagnosis is the core of the facility that monitors and maintains a person's records, medical status, operations, medicine, and therapies. All operations are performed using a variety of devices that use robotic intelligence, from the microscopic to a level of surgical methods not known today. The use of sound and color therapies has advanced through the discovery of ancient Egyptian, Indian and Chinese texts that have proven invaluable in the treatment of many forms of physical, emotional, and mental deficiencies. The term *disease* is no longer used, for it was determined to be a form of false identification. Issues in the future will deal with deficiencies. The energy of a person will be the telling sign of deficiencies or imbalances. Medicines will rely more on their natural attributes than those manufactured by chemical manipulation. The holistic concepts will be enhanced so that our current understanding will be deemed archaic. The cloning of anything, as I mentioned before, will be abolished. If it does not have a divine spark, it will not be allowed.

The use of governments will change. The world will have a ruling body made up of twelve wise men and women. Young adults will sit on a lower panel based on the wisdom they exhibit. The ruling body will apply order as it pertains to the health of the planet and its people. Local councils will also have some influence, but their role will be to make sure the distribution of food and other services is flowing smoothly. The rare disputes that arise between neighbors will be addressed and resolved by that ruling district. I should add that there will be no such thing as kings, queens, presidents, or representatives. Those who are in positions of authority are voted in by local populations who cast their votes through technology that does not exist today. There is no such thing as a term limit. If people are doing their jobs according to their assigned roles, they stay. The moment their performance does not meet the standards of their position, they are replaced. This is not a problem, because all officials understand their role and the levels of responsibility they are expected to achieve. This is true of many roles in this future society.

The vanguard of future activity is to be the preservation of life on Earth. The tectonic plates have begun to move more dynamically. The loss of most of the ice shelves has had a dramatic impact on many species of the planet. Weather conditions have gone from extreme to more moderate conditions; the sun's impact on life has changed. Mankind must protect himself in more unique ways because of the sun's increased activity. Because of the earthly changes, mankind has had to adapt to react faster to severe weather and earthly conditions. This has required more cooperation from far-flung corners of Earth and the use of more mobile equipment with skilled robots and technicians. They use life-saving devices that can provide shelter, clothing, and food for a significant number of people and animals at one time. The world has evolved and is still evolving.

Mankind is using robotics of the day in new and more dynamic ways. The use of artificial intelligence is now controlled because of the rapid rise of uses that created more problems than anyone at the time could have imagined. The role of mankind is in a state of evolution from the historic to a level of consciousness that can be described as elevated and expanded. The true meaning of this is written in the stars. It is written in a way that only becomes apparent when mankind awakens to his role in what is to be.

The Corridor of Time

L ike all journeys, this one begins somewhere. This journey begins now. Its starting point is wherever you are in the present moment. From a broad overview, mankind is in the now of time and space. Humans are in a corridor of time as they transition from one place or state of awareness to another. The way this journey goes is seemingly without a plan or a destination. Why is this moment a journey without a plan or destination?

Look around. Check every aspect of life as you know it. Do you have a plan for your life's journey? If you do, you are blessed. Now, as you look around, does it appear that others are as blessed? The ancients say that there is a plan, and it is filled with beauty and joy. However, on the surface, most of us see confusion, chaos, and random acts of violence. We see a sense of mindlessness, not purpose. So what is important about the corridor of time? The flow of wisdom from a greater source indicates that we are in the throes of change, from climate to politics to the use of drugs for recreational use, to advancing technology and shifting relationships. Change is a constant, and it is accelerating. Now is the time to look at a possible direction, based not on past practices but on the question "What if?"

The transition appears to be like none that has come before. It's a form of transformation of human thought. It involves the application of life as a gift of divine sources. This is like a corridor of transition in time. I use the term *corridor* to symbolize the sense of direction. Nowhere does mankind see an overriding direction of his conscious application of existence. The movement of advancements in technology, science, medicine, and social interaction is seen as progress. The truth of progress is an increase and enhancement of conscious awareness, the striving to learn about the inner light that guides the inner abilities of creation, and the establishment of harmony both within and without, linked not just to self but also to the core of existence. Aggrandizement of the ego is not harmony created or experienced. Knowledge of the sacredness of life and the application of that knowledge are the keys to advancement locally and globally.

The corridor of time is the use of a symbol that most people can either visualize or identify with. Time is a known or accepted reality of third-dimensional thinking. The corridor and time are used as experience generators. The symbol of the corridor indicates direction, and visualization and time are the keepers of cycles and relationships to identify location of consciousness. The truth is that neither exists in advanced states of consciousness. The issue is this: How do we move from present states of awareness and beliefs to the next step?

How about the creation of a new template for conscious application of the gifts of life?

Let us ponder this issue for a moment. The issue is based on current knowledge, beliefs, and history. It is based on the DNA of accepted models of experience and expected results. As difficult as this may be to accept, all of us are one collective consciousness, one collective energy that accepts separation, duality, and impermanence. The challenges of mankind are many, but the greatest challenge is one of dominance. Mankind falls into two main groups: those who seek to conquer or win at any level and those who accept that they are just here to be, whatever that means. It is a form of separation of those who have and those who have not. The rite of passage that mankind goes through is one of trials and tribulations. This extends from one end of the globe to the other. Mankind has even imagined a God who is vengeful and destructive, judges, and favors one group or concept of spirituality over another. The knowledge of the ancients is hidden or destroyed to satisfy the nature of man's willingness to dominate. The structure of life is set to punish in ways untold. Now we are asked to ponder the issue of current consciousness versus what comes next.

The answer is complex to those who do not understand the nature of truth. Here is a suggestion. Let the information coming forth be received with an open mind.

What If

- Mankind was asked to accept the fact that all humans came from one seed? One concept of creation?
- Mankind was given a new way to communicate with his god or gods without someone telling him how, why, or when?
- Mankind was told the only difference between humans was a matter of gender?
- Mankind was taught from childhood that life is a gift to explore all he can envision and beyond and that the world is a garden of creation when truly understood?
- Love of life was the way to journey the path of existence, and the only enemy of fate is not having faith in your creative nature?
- All humans stood on the mountaintops of the world and attempted to hold hands, and each and every person could actually touch another by holding hands?
- Mankind realized that death was a transition into another form of life and that the longer people live, the greater the chance they will achieve the greatness they possess?
- Mankind was taught to respect the differences in life and not judge them as inferior or superior to one another and to understand that life is equally distributed as long as there is breath?

- Mankind chooses the language of love instead of a language of hate, understanding that all words are thoughts and beliefs eventually made manifest?
- Mankind was taught that *I* was not a designation of separation but a complex of human interaction and that the *I* in "I AM" is symbolic for "We ARE"?
- Mankind realized through the wisdom of the ancients that we are part of nature; a unifying force, not a disruptive one; and not just a single spark but a flame that illuminates the world?
- Mankind was given a road map to a new reality?

Would mankind take such an opportunity? I think not, because the foundation for conscious change has not been set.

A New Template
in the Corridors of Time

Based on my business experience, I understand what it takes to build a company, but beginning a work that could lead an entire world to a new level of thought is monumental. At least that was my initial impression, and then I thought of something I wrote to myself several months ago: "Know that no one person can be responsible for the ultimate transition of man, but one person among many can start the train of transformation of consciousness."

How do we set the foundation of the change we think has to take place? First, my prayer is that we are in accord with the will of the divine and that what I write and share is for the highest good of mankind. My intention is to raise the consciousness of mankind in love and light without end. Amen. Ho.

The game of life of one is a game of life of many; it is the game of life of all. The game is more real than you think and calls for new guidelines. The following is a set of guidelines that can be enhanced through the use of progressive and intuitive thought. This is the moment of thought in alignment with the concepts of right, heartfelt thinking. May the words follow divine will.

This is what I received: darkness leads to light. The journey to the truth is one taken by all of the creative on Earth. How the journey goes is up to the free will of each and every spark of life. Ignorance of truth is a disregard for the reality embedded in existence. No one person is the savior of the world; only God has dominion over all. The spark of life indwells in everyone. The existence of this spark is not currently taught as fact but as an ideal. Nowhere is love more prevalent than in the heart of one who is open to the gift of compassion. There is no greater gift than to love one another unconditionally. The form love takes is beyond description when it originates from the Source of creation. Now is not only a gift but also an opportunity. The time to reveal your inner self begins now. No moment is as important as this moment to decide your future. Past rewards both positive and negative, from a judgment standpoint, are from the source of your beliefs. Change your beliefs by being willing to change yourself. Set your course of future events by believing in the higher aspect of your will to do the right thing. Allow your mind to be silent, and listen more closely to the wisdom of the heart. Let your past stay there. Do not bring your baggage with you as you journey now through life. Be in this moment, one with the realization that you are a gift. Open it gently.

Now, in this moment, there is momentum. Space is the absolute dimension where momentum is experienced or felt. In this moment, there is momentum to change in significant ways. This means the winds of change have shifted and are no longer resistant to change. There is a flow, an ease associated with the dynamic of change. This could be viewed as both good and bad. The good is an enabler of changing habits and accepted beliefs of modern man and his consciousness. The bad is the lack of understanding as to what is taking place and how to, in effect, navigate the times. This is where the corridor of time resides. Make no mistake: no one is left out of this experience. The only question is how one interprets what is taking place. The myriad of options are as numerous as the stars. Completion of the task at hand allows many to experience a higher form of expression, but *completion* is just a word to describe a higher form of life's potential.

Working now with the corridor of time is an opportunity to realize and connect with the world of cause. This opportunity is like lifting the consciousness above the current level of awareness to a higher vibration or octave. Using more of one's awareness brings knowledge that is right below the surface of consciousness as it is currently accepted and experienced. Making one an expression of absolute potential is not the panacea that is of the fantasy world. Potential is not a form of mastery but an opportunity to realize what one's true capabilities are, if left to the vista of an open heart and mind. Combine the two aspects of human function (heart and mind) with the love of the divine, and observe what can materialize in this space of third-dimensional existence.

More of life is not a limiter to others. It is an enabler to others in the form of radiant examples. The corridor of time is now an open magnet to hope. How you enter the corridor has been preordained by the fate of the star structure you were born under or within. Right now, is the beginning of the journey. How should we approach our entry or our travel through the structure of time and space?

1) How prepared are you to change from the current role you have accepted as you or yours?
2) What is your belief in the power of a force greater than you?
3) When you look at the mirror of existence, do you see a person who is the captain of his or her fate or destiny?
4) What is the current feeling you have in the pit of your stomach?
5) Are you connected to that feeling at all?
6) Have you ever asked yourself why you are here?
7) Have you ever gotten an answer? If so, what was it?
8) Do you believe you are the product of your beliefs?
9) Can you list your beliefs?
10) How often do you pray for a better life for you and for others?
11) Who do you believe created the you that you are? Do you feel, or have you ever felt, you were that creator or co-creator?
12) What is the nature of the words you use to communicate your thoughts and feelings?
13) In your inner and intimate thoughts, do you think or feel you can be more than who you currently are?

I suggest you answer and record these thirteen questions. If you look back at these questions at some future point in time, you will see what was and what is and have an idea of what can be.

How far have you come in what you call personal progress? How far have you come in reaching what you desire? Is your goal inches or miles away? Realize that what you desire is within. This may be obvious to some, but to many, it is not a form their consciousness takes. This is now a problem of mass consciousness. The problem is the desire to have something you already have. The explanation is as follows:

- The heart of mankind is not involved in that which is consciousness raised.
- The mind of mankind is involved in a race to reach something that is out there.
- The focus of man is based on time and space, leading to a requirement of unending desire.
- That which is desire is based on something other than what one believes one has.
- Those who focus on the realm of manifestation do not realize the role they play in manifesting current reality.
- The part one plays appears to be independent of those that came before and will come after.
- Those who seek the limits of their expression are few but growing.
- One by one, humans will find that their path is evolving.
- The time this takes is presently speeding up.
- Those who progress will choose many doors before new visions will be available based on focus.
- The light of divine essence will shine brightly on those who release the old forms of completion.
- No one will move forward faster than those who breathe the light of conscious transition (faster as in speed in this case is not related to time).

What is progress? In this situation, it is the level of consciousness you embrace. Each level is perfect for the level of consciousness you are currently at. No one is misplaced. One's focus, called a life plan, leads one to travel the path of creation. What makes a difference is knowledge. Sacred knowledge flows at a level that is not only sacred but also the realization that all things are sacred when the divine spark is revealed. How do we move from one level of consciousness to another? We pass through the portals of acceleration and evolve. How do we participate in this seeming elevation?

Progress in the Conscious Application of Self

Elevation is a matter of vibration. One speeds up and slows down periodically over the course of a lifetime. When one accepts the responsibility of creation, one realizes the truth of great proportion. Nowhere does mankind accept the totality of his relationship to this truth. We are creations of divine will. That will allow for separation on one hand and infinite diversity on the other. That will has also granted us free will as a way to experience and grow in the third dimension. One does the creating. What does that mean? It is the reflection of the one Source to create. We as a band of creative intelligence have lost the realization that the Source of our message is the one within us. It is the one Source within All.

The process of elevation is not like going up in an elevator. It is revealing to the inner world that your intention is to find the center where the will of mind and will of heart are linked, a place of receptivity where truth is allowed to reveal itself. The focus on the inner realm of heart and mind in a state of receptivity creates a relationship that begins to open many doors that have been allowed by the limited truth of one's creation to be concealed. This connectivity takes practice and dedication, but in this time-space illusion, there is an opportunity like none before for mass consciousness to grasp the truths that dwell in the Mind of Creation. The way to clearer perception of reality is at hand. The question is no longer if but when we will raise our consciousness and potential up to levels we have little understanding of now.

The heart of hearts within us seeks the knowledge to pursue the absolute in all things. Seek ye now the kingdom of the divine, seeking in a way in which the heart leads and the mind follows. This is not a course in miracles (which has already been written); it is the path of creative potential. The limits on current knowledge are based on our beliefs. It is a result of cause and effect on mass consciousness. It is what evolution is all about. How do you move past the results of existing norms?

The answer lies in achieving a greater understanding of what one's responsibility is individually and collectively. Awaken to the light of transition as it moves through the cycles and rhythms of mankind and his world. Take steps to realize what exists for all beings of Earth. Realize that all that was is illusion, and all that is is illusion, not from the standpoint of experience but from the perception of a desire to grow as a life force on Earth. Unity of mind and heart brings one closer to a realization that there is more to this experience than isolated thinking and being. The opening of the heart and the receptivity of mind join with the spirit of being to create a new path of experience and expression.

A Time of Transition

This is a moment of extraordinary change. This is a moment in time when mankind crosses the level of consciousness that has allowed expression to take place in a limited range of understanding. What mankind sees as opportunity of conscious evolution, Godkind sees as the moment of transition. How is this explained?

Mankind has evolved to a plateau of latent understanding, a level where conscious creation meets the realm of possibilities. In terms of those who choose to evolve, this is important. "The sky's the limit" is an old saying meant to demonstrate that what is holds open-ended potential. The truth, however, is that when one sees the sky, he or she sees the illusion of third-dimensional thought and the acceptance of reality as it appears. There is not an opening to explore the realms of higher consciousness. This comment does not take in all beings of third-dimensional existence. Are there those who choose concepts above the limits of this realm? Absolutely. But how many are there? Not many.

The realm of conscious acceptance of what is moves as the stars move. There is always movement. That is the basis for creation. All that lives moves in a rhythm dictated by the fundamental laws of cause and effect. Nowhere does manifestation take place without movement in the rhythm of correspondence. This rhythm is absolute based on creation's life and lessons. The consciousness of one is embraced by the many. This is the limit placed on man. He has accepted the limits imposed by separation from his life source, from essence. This acceptance is self-limiting and, as a result, limiting in a range that is accepted as real. This dream presents one with a dilemma. What would it take to wake up, and how many would it take to release us from the dream? It takes an awareness that the dream, as presently constituted, is by its very nature restrictive. It takes a desire to learn the true nature of being and of potential. The number it would take is a variable based on knowledge that is not available to this writer. My belief is that it would take critical mass based on the overall energy invested in the third dimension.

What comes now is a moment in time, the opportunity to expand the bounds of this illusion or break them completely. How fortunate is this moment? How do we begin to move forward? The answer lies in trust. It lies in the ability to trust that there is something greater than the collective consciousness of mankind: The Source of All There Is. Because we choose to personalize something that is beyond mortal comprehension, we reverently refer to this Source as God.

The covenant of creation is not a myth; it is the reality and progression of life. Movement now is in the direction of what I will term *refinement*. One definition that has come to me is that *refinement is*, "the art of intelligence gathering". Another definition is from Webster's College Dictionary, "a subtle point or distinction. An improved form of something". This movement will allow mankind to extend the boundaries of life as we know it. It will place a burden on those who move forward in life's stream, not in the form of destruction but in the form of release. What has been will not be. What has been accepted as reality will shift in many ways, and what was considered dear in the form of material expressions of comfort and success will fade as a result of the energies of refinement.

The movement of mankind through the tunnel he is now in will seem to be confining for some and liberating for others. The choice of the drama and of existence itself is up to each and every soul. Now comes the good part: How do we play in this game of life when the rules appear about to change?

I'll give the answer in a moment. First, there is a need to understand what is, so we can determine what will be.

The current moment possesses light—the light of the concept of individualized self, a concept of illusion when realized for what it is. This is now a place of unlimited potential and unlimited learning about life and its true rewards. This is the moment when the focus of self-deception is identified. What is creation, and who are its participants?

Life is creation, and we are its participants. What is the connection? Life is the creative spark in all that manifests in time and space and beyond. Life is a matrix of energy that is both magnetic and filled with force. Life does not exist without a reason, and that reason supersedes logic. Life is a blend of absolutes and potential. Life begins in the unmanifest as a pure state and moves to complete itself without judgment. Life precedes the thought of separation but binds that thought in a form of attraction that is the result of cause and effect. All life is a gift of joy, but the gift is not understood.

Mankind is the manifestation of like thinking. Mankind is an expression of the potential of life itself. Mankind participates in life with a knowing of his place in the universe. This knowing is concealed by the husk of self-identification. This game of self-deception is preordained by concepts magnified by a collective whole—by a consciousness that states the *I* is more powerful than the *we*, by the acceptance that the creative force simply is but is ignored, and by the lack of light provided to wake up the slumbering consciousness of man. Mankind participates in creation without the foundation of understanding the gift of creation and his role in it.

The light of awareness shines dimly at this time based on man's preoccupation with the present circumstances of life. This acceptance of that which is is based on the memory of a bygone time. It is based on historical cycles and the traditions built up over time. The reason and cause for current conscious levels of awareness are based on past cycles of concepts that have been accepted as reality and truth. The time-space continuum of existing practices is a fixed complex of thoughts, beliefs, and accepted norms. The time of realized self-denial is at hand.

What do I mean by self-denial? Look out at the lives of others, and see your relationship to them. Look out at world activities, and identify your position within those activities. Look in a mirror, and ask what do you see. Listen now to your heart. What, if anything, do you hear? Listen to your mind. What are the thoughts you have carried for years? How often do thoughts seem to appear in your mind that make you ask consciously, "Where did that come from?" Can you sense how hard or soft your heart is? When you reach out your hand, what do you see? How aware are you of the life streams that cross your path? When was the last time you paid attention to your breath? What am I getting at?

What is self-denial? It is the face you put on based on your present state of awareness. It is a game of life you play when you are with someone or alone. It is the moment you open your eyes and accept that which is normal. It is the opening of a new day, as if it were yesterday. You might say, "I still don't understand." What is self-denial?

It is the acceptance of self as a cause of anything. It is the identification you have placed on yourself as a citizen of any group, a concept that does not demonstrate the full range of your capacity to achieve the wonders of life. In effect, it is the identity that does not love without some form of stimulation. It is the fact that you identify with your material form and not your spiritual content.

How do we move to a new level of consciousness? The issue is great. The move to a new level of consciousness is based on an openness to accept the greater aspect residing within. This requires an internal commitment that is steadfast and focused. It also requires a willingness to forgive all things, including all things that came before. Be aware that forgiveness is one of the most fundamental powers of love. It is the willingness to be all you can be. There are no downward thoughts of what was or upward thoughts of a supreme judge, just a focus and commitment to the now, to that which is currently present. Forgiveness takes an open mind, open heart, and willing soul. It's not easy but is available when desire meets love.

The essence of divine love guides the way when one chooses the path of light. This is a choice of infinite possibilities. The path of light that now enters the spectrum of Earth's existence is like a light in the tunnel of one's creative mind. The openness that one creates is based on the internal desire to move from the confines of one's acceptance of what seems currently available to what is beyond the spectrum of one's beliefs. Opening the mind to receive sounds simple, but the mind that accepts the current state of affairs is not easily persuaded to change. The heart of all that exists opens and closes to what it perceives as love and what it perceives as danger. When one finds the soul, he or she is unified in thought and in perception with what exists in the current state and potential future states of evolution. The soul shows the way for some, for it knows the direction of the lessons to be learned. This process is one where some are easily linked or in tune with their soul while the majority of us have a tendency to ignore or overlook the aspect of self that is in tune with the urgings of the soul.

When one opens the mind, he or she must first find the kernel of existence in the heart that directs the rays of illumination and awareness. This kernel resides within. There is no "out there" when the truth is so close at hand. The mind will follow when it feels that the falseness of its perception is revealed. An open mind and heart come from a state of acceptance of a higher aspect of creation. One must be present to tune in to what is not real but what is true.

Have you stood at a doorway and hesitated for a moment before entering? Or have you stood at a door and hesitated before leaving your home, office, or place of work? If the answer is yes, then you realize that something or someone created that hesitation. This moment calls for a similar hesitation. The doorway you are about to transition through is a change in the momentum of life, the way to a new form of consciousness that calls for awareness and a desire for something beyond the visual. It calls for something different.

This is a transition of conscious intent. It looks like a change from normalcy to interrupted thinking. What is interrupted thinking?

It is a revision in the template of conscious thought. Each thought is like an energy wave. It has peaks and valleys. It is linear in nature, and it is energy. Now you think your thoughts come without much effort. That is a state of conscious sleeping. You are on autopilot, if you will. You are asleep to the reality you create with your thoughts. This is nothing new. It has been going on for eons. It is a form of flatline thinking. This means you are unaware of the power of your thoughts, which are generated from the foundation of the beliefs you hold as real. The flatline is ignoring your current state of awareness in the process of creating your reality. The moment of experience is also the moment of acceptance. You accept what you create as experience. This form of existence is not abnormal; it is absolutely accepted as normal.

What does this mode of creation get you? It is the simplicity of existence, and it allows for the rhythm of life to be maintained in what seems to be an orderly sequence. The problem exists at the crossroads of life humanity has accepted as truth. This truth is not as simple as one would accept. The existing truth is that life is seen as separate, something apart from nature and from the spirit of existence. Life is the *I*, and life is seen through the eyes of the ego. This is the accepted truth, and it is the shell of human endeavor. This is an acceptance of life that now needs to be identified. The *I* in the human condition is a belief in the individual nature of all things. I am a part (as in separate), and I am unique, but I am not part of any consciousness, because all I accept is my individual space. Ah, space—it is the separator. It is the isolator. It is a reason for the acceptance of *I* as separate from the whole. It is your willingness to see distance and accept separation as a form of reality. The folly of third-dimensional thinking, belief, and experience is the reason for day becoming night.

The following comes from a higher realm of thought that does not identify with the concept of what the term *I* in our present state of awareness accepts as reality. The word *I* is not being defined using our normal terms or level of understanding.

No amount of words will clarify the situation of modern man and the word *I*. *I* is not meant to precede anything. *I* is not a follower of the truth. *I* does not exist as an independent entity. *I* is meant to be understood in a greater context. It is the truth to say, "I have a purpose." What is that purpose? It is to demonstrate unity. The *I* of light is the universe of creation. Light is meant to convey the messages of love, not the romantic kind but the love of creation and harmony with the laws of the divine. If the dawn of awakened consciousness is to be realized, then this truth has to be understood and experienced now. There appears to be an *I* that is identified as the ego and an *I* of the greater self. The *I* we experience in day-to-day living relates to mind and the associations of third-dimensional concepts. There is a greater aspect of who we are that knows there is more than our current perceptions.

The focus of now is to awaken the consciousness of mankind to the truth within thought. The direction one takes in life is based on the focus, vibration, and rhythm within thought. If you seek thought that separates, you have distance and the lack of caring. If you seek thoughts that unify, you enter into a dynamic of giving. One separates, and one unifies. What is the difference? Focus, intent, and the rhythm of thought. Now we come to a threshold. We come to the doorway of what appears as an opportunity. Hesitate for a moment longer if you will, but the dynamics of change are upon the horizons of life.

Once life begins, there is a stream of consciousness. This stream is unique to the individual and to the life path one leads. There is significance to life. It is meant to grow in the direction dictated by one's soul intent. Once life begins, there is a carrier of thought and expression: the personality. The direction and intent of life appear to be directed by the circumstances of life and the models of behavior one accepts as real. The truth of existence appears to be one of trial and error, one of going forth and then experiencing the trials of life. Each soul is given a task, and each task fits a plan of creation. Although many things appear random, the reality is that life is lived according to law. This means that for every cause, there is an effect. It also means that awareness and responsibility of action are the right of every life on Earth. This is the way of things now and always. The meaning of *right* flows with an attachment, if you will. That attachment states that one grows through experience and expression. What one reaps is what one sows. The meaning is covered in layers. To ponder is to give pause to allow a greater form of understanding to come forth from inner realms. There is a great deal embedded in this information. It is up to us to lift the veil to realize the knowledge and wisdom that we possess.

The crossroads of existence now calls for awareness and responsibility. It calls for an understanding of what life is and is not. Trouble in any language is the responsibility of the land of creation in which adventure and misadventure take place. *Trouble* is not a word of fear. It is a word of creation. Do not place yourself in harm's way to prove valor or worthiness. The truth of seeking change is not to seek trouble. It is not to extend yourself beyond the realm of your awareness. It is to seek the road of clarity on which one is to travel. Now comes the moment to adhere to the thought of change within the canopy of Earth's experience. How do we move forward with the limited understanding we now have?

The process is lacking without knowledge. How do we gain the knowledge necessary to move forward past the crossroads of current consciousness? How do we realize the moment is one of opportunity and not trouble?

Forget for a moment that you exist as an individual on this sphere of organic matter. Forget that you have come through the birth canal to breathe life as an idea in your mind and in the minds of others. You might say, "How do I do that? I am conscious of my existence here and now. I know who I am, and I know who I have been. How do I forget all of that? I know those with dementia and Alzheimer's have that issue, but I cannot forget who I am." Then I have another request. Forget who gave you the gift of life. I am not referring to your parents. How many of you remember who gave you the gift of life? I do not mean the thought of a religious concept. I mean the remembrance of that which you are. I mean the spark of intelligence and creative thought that you are. This is not a game. The truth is that the vast majority of the citizens of this world do not remember their origination as a part of life. We are one with all life; how many remember that? How many know that? Once more, I ask that you forget that you exist as an individual on Earth and are an idea in the mind of creation.

By attempting this exercise, you are attempting to reorient yourself to the way of life as it is to be in the future. You are evolving your thought process, even if only for a moment. The focus on self is essential in the beginning to awaken your gift of awareness. This focus is complete when one realizes each moment as unique and as an opportunity to rise above the current state of mind. Awareness is focus. Focus is the concentration of energy on the play of life. Now is focus, not tomorrow or yesterday. Now is focus. Life moves, and you observe. Observe now in two directions: externally on the play of life and internally on the dynamic of your interpretation of life. Both are important, but one has a greater impact than the other. The internal game is strong, powerful, and all creative. The external appears as a result of the internal process.

The gift of life is twofold. If you're open to your creative inspiration, you receive the reward of knowing your success. Some call it their passion in life. If you're closed to your inner wellspring of your purpose, the trials and tribulations of life are experienced at different levels and accepted in different ways. One way is adaptable, and the other is not. The way to the gift of life is through a process I will call love. First, what is the gift of life? It is the possibility that you are in existence. It is the creative life force that is. It is a consciousness unfolding. It is the light of heaven about to be revealed. All that you are is an attempt to bring forth the mind of creation, not as an isolated spark in a field of nothing but as a force of divine energy in the field of creation. Your gift is not you, but it is you a thousand-fold.

Let the light of awareness bring forth a new relationship with the external of life and the internal spark of your creative nature.

Awareness calls for commitment, not in the future but in the present moment.

Awareness calls for commitment to observe that which is within and that which appears separate from self.

Awareness calls for a sense of refinement, not in your outer garment but in your role as a gift of the creative in all things.

Awareness calls for the way to be cleared of old, worn-out beliefs.

Awareness is an opportunity to change not through force but through letting go of restrictive thoughts and ideals.

This is not a step-by-step process. All of awareness is in the doing, but it is not doing at all. It is being still, quieting the mind, and releasing the blinders of habitual rituals you live every day. Awareness is alignment of energy in that you focus your attention on life. This requires not only focus and intent now but also the letting go of the mechanism in time.

Conquer now the fear of being in the position you are meant to be in. You have an image of self in the confines of third-dimensional thinking. This image is based on the judgment of self, the judgment of others, and the level of acceptance you want from the world. You have placed yourself in the world based on your beliefs of the world. Many of your beliefs have set you in the place where you now find yourself. This is not the reality you choose but the reality that appears to have chosen you. You are the product of the reality that provides you the ability to create at a level of your current consciousness. The issue is that nothing is wrong. There is no right or wrong for the life you have created. It is what it is. The lessons are yours, and you find a way to make them appear real.

Now is an opportunity to realize the power of your creative self. There is one attribute that has been left out of your will to live life fully: connectivity, not as a lifeline or a support structure but as a form of relationship that is neutral in scope and reaction. You are a spark of life, and as such, you have a gift to explore the infinite in all things. How does that work with connectivity?

You are a canvas of unlimited creativity. Your brushstroke is sure and brilliant. Then another brushstroke is created by another hand. How did this happen, when this is your canvas? Your blank canvas turned out to be someone else's canvas as well. You just did not realize it. Now there are two brushstrokes. Wait—another brushstroke has just appeared. Something is going on here. What was yours appears as something for many people to paint on. What is the lesson here? The lesson is to realize you do not create in a vacuum. You are part of a great mosaic that is ever-evolving. This mosaic is not part of our present consciousness due to our acceptance of self. The truth is that the canvas of life is filled with different colors, hues, and strokes and we are the artists. They all blend. Some clash, and others overlap, but they fill out the picture in an ever-evolving creative process.

Connectivity is the way of future endeavors, a way of change. How does this change take place? It takes place by attention to what is driving change. What is driving this change is part of a cycle of evolution—not physical evolution but conscious evolution. Conscious evolution in what way? What makes mankind unique? Humans have dominion over all they survey. They grow in technology, in raising their own food, and in taking care of their societal and health-care needs. They also believe in spiritual and religious practices, and they evolve their needs to accommodate the vehicles that provide their day-to-day lives. They also conduct war and destruction on one another for any reason they can concoct. Life is not seen as a gift; it is seen as a burden or not seen at all. In this time, we can contribute to our conscious evolution by becoming aware of a greater sense that we are part of something greater. Something that is not ornamental but a living breathing dynamic that requires us to be aware of our beliefs and our judgements not just of one another but of the creative force that exists within. It is time for a conscious shift in priorities as we dwell in the space of our third-dimensional birth.

The game of life is in a state of flux. A state of transition from what is perceived as normal to what is seen as potential. The game of life is based on our acceptance and our beliefs. What comes next is the opportunity to create a vision for yourself that does not apply the concept of limits. When you wake tomorrow set your expectations of life up a little. See more flexibility in what comes your way. Look for options to your present circumstances that you feel good about. Check your beliefs about who you are by being aware of how you react to existing situations. Are you worthy of a life that is more abundant and harmonious? See the triangle of faith, trust and gratitude as a way to formulate a plan for your future (see section faith, trust and gratitude). Allow your energy to focus on yourself and those around you in a loving way. Pray, meditate and contemplate using words that are uplifting and not denying or limiting. Give yourself time to realize that you are willing to change, in accordance with the changes taking place around you. Love yourself in a way that allows others to love you. Be at peace and begin to realize that you are and have never been alone. You are part of a great matrix and that matrix would not exist without you.

Change requires diligence, commitment and courage. It is not accomplished in a day, so be kind to yourself and be patient.

The Rest of the Story

That which is brings forth the vision of a new life from the forms of expression that exist today. The journey of man through the labyrinth of experience has been, from the concepts of time and space, a long and arduous journey. Mankind's acceptance of life as a model of survival has been challenging. The roles that man has chosen to play have yielded forms of harmony and discord. The tendency to survive at almost any cost has been destructive to the lives of those involved and to the planet and life-forms that have accepted their roles within creation. The dawning of a new concept of being has been repeated several times in the past with uplifting results. Those times have seen expansion and then, as the purity of the message decays, a contraction. Now, as has been stated before, mankind is at a crossroads. The result is open to the creative expression within man. The future is a blank canvas as seen through the eyes and minds of the creative within third-dimensional vision. The truth is that mankind must evolve of his own efforts for the canvas of creation to be filled with a full spectrum of life and its potential.

The way forward in this material covers the recent past, the state of the present as it applies to this sharing, and the future as seen through the eyes of a vision that has the real potential to be. Covering the journey of so many souls is a challenge, one that has been accepted in the light it is given. The material covers the impediments on the journey of so many by focusing on the critical reasons for darkness to be the forms of existence that have been and are the expressions and experiences as you have known them.

So what comes next? What is the rest of the story?

Preparation is important. Each life brings to the current moment a reservoir of knowledge and experience. Each life is here in the now for a reason. Each soul born now and existing now has a reason for being. Every breath one takes leads to the next step, the next thought, and the next word one will speak. Each and every breath is a result of some influence that came before. Each breath, when seen from above the landscape of existing consciousness, is the culmination of something that came before. Notice your breath and, with a clear mind, just observe. What kind of breath did you just take? Was it short, deep, hurried, anxious, frightened, relaxed, or restricted? Now look back to just a moment before, and see if you can recognize what preceded the breath. It might be difficult, because you were in the process of reading or hearing this material. But choose a time, any time, to watch your breath, and observe what preceded it. The reason for this is to verify the information and knowledge this material is imparting.

The breath you take, and the breath that each person in the world takes individually and collectively, is a result of something that just took place. If the breath of the individual and the breath of the world are affected by the same thing, does that not raise the question of what else impacts all of us? If we are influenced or react one way, is there a possibility that the sum of our parts creates something on a level that we are not consciously aware of? The answer is just one example of the underlying unity of man.

What are some other examples? When ancient men drew themselves up from slumber, they saw something of significance in the sky. The sun shone brightly on most of their days. Their body chemistry reacted in a certain way. The cadence of their functions responded according to the rising and setting of the sun. Today we work from morning to morning. The advent of pills and stimulants allows for a wide variety of responses, but when viewed from the natural process, our bodies respond in much the same way our ancestors' bodies did.

The focus of the light within our eyes is in a range where, for most, perception is experienced. When darkness falls due to the absence of sunlight, our reaction to the dark is universal. Most of us cannot see in the dark. The blind among us have accustomed themselves to the lack of sight as best as they can and have developed other senses to a heightened degree. Those of us who can see find the darkness challenging. Many feel—and have experienced— negative things because of darkness. Why do most of us respond to darkness in the same way? Is there something within that triggers this mechanism?

The role of mankind is not unique within the context of life as a universal concept. What is unique is the level of impact darkness, or lack of light, has on our challenges. We are within the realm of creative thinking. Our experience of this process has led us to evolve in an uneven manner. There have been prior civilizations that have journeyed through the mist of time with limited ability to evolve past a certain level of expression.

One of the most difficult concepts to overcome is that diversity means difference. This has led to clashes of intellect, spirituality, and self-preservation, which have resulted in stagnation and displacement. The time is here to arrive at a new destination in thought, ideals, and expression of free will. Defining life is not easy. The changing of the concepts of current reality from a fixed position to one of observation, willingness to learn, and release of existing beliefs is, to say the least, challenging. The way forward seeks to introduce concepts that will facilitate a beginning to a lifelong process of conscious evolution.

The current moment is one of self-examination. Ask yourself, "Where do I rest when surrounded by my beliefs? Do I question anything about my life, my direction in life, or the results my beliefs have generated in my life? Am I a seeker? Do I thirst for knowledge, or do I accept that which is told to me? How often do I break the barriers of my habits? Do I seek a better life for myself and those I love, or do I accept my fate in the circumstances of my life?" This may surprise you, but both sides of our questions are acceptable. Both sides of the balance of life are divine. There is nothing right or wrong with either expression. There is a perfection in expression that is not easily understood or accepted by our belief and judgment systems.

The hue and cry will be "What about terrorists, mass murderers, child molesters, and random acts of violence? What about disease and the loss of children due to illness or accidents?" The answer seems complex. What can be forgiven, and what can be accepted as divine will or plan? To the mind of mass consciousness, these things cannot be justified. To the villains in the event, their justifications are valid. Their right is someone else's wrong. The reality is that the destruction of life comes from lack of sight, loss of knowledge, and use of will in the ways of duality. The acceptance of wars and dominance of any kind is the displacement of love for any other thing you can name. Extremism in anything calls for balance. The law of cause and effect is absolute. If that is the case, then how is anything of darkness justified? It isn't, but our judgment adds to the game of life as it is currently being expressed. The right thing is not what you think. "An eye for an eye and a tooth for a tooth" is not love in action. It is the law of cause and effect being played out without knowledge and awareness. The nature of what is taking place calls for awareness. To change the flow of action and reaction requires understanding that the duality embedded in this world provides choices. There are a couple questions here: How do we release the imbalances of our world? What can we do to make this place a place restored to a higher and more harmonious order of things?

Realize that in this moment, you are the opportunity to bring about change. Your thoughts, actions, and desires are the basis for a new now. Your energy is here for a reason, and through your actions, you can create a better tomorrow. The how is based on your life path and the direction you feel good about. Each person has a calling, and when people align themselves with that direction, there is a knowing that can be described as joy. For each and every one, there is a plan. That plan is unique to each soul on Earth. Bring harmony to your ideals by realizing that the life force within awaits your recognition.

The house of God, the Creator, the Source, houses all. The righteous are there by design, by their actions. Those who think they are above the law of divine right action learn in due order the truth of existence. Thus, we move to a level where the role of the individual will now be seen in a different light. If you think you have the answer, you're right when you realize you are part of a greater whole, your contributions matter, and your actions release the confines of the age of transition. Transition is a process, and you are not only part of the process; you are the process.

The way forward is open to those who seek a higher form of expression. The breath you take and the role you play are part of the creation of life. Open your mind and heart to a message that states, "This world is your world, and as such, it is now open to accept your highest effort through conscious acceptance of the love you are." Peace.

Rather than the End, a Beginning

We are in a continuum of existence. We are the product of evolution, and as such, we are, in essence, an expression of creation. We have moved the dial of consciousness and existence forward in what appears a short time based on Earth's calendar. That process is speeding up due to factors that have been discussed in this material. The reality is that we are going through change, and this will continue as we move forward in time and space. I have attempted to take this moment to summarize what is taking place. The information received to write this summary has taken on a different complexion than what I originally planned, but I have learned through this process to tune in to what is coming through and write as this stream of consciousness is being received.

For every man, woman, and child, there is a season to yearn for completion. For every man, woman, and child, there is a time to evolve in the direction of his or her birthright and soul's journey. For us all, there is a time to breathe and a time to hear the true nature of what is taking place. Now, at this time, we have experienced without consciously realizing it a form of energy (my interpretation) from a distant place: the celestial event that came from the constellation of Cygnus. With my limited knowledge, the only way I have to describe it is that it was energy of a higher vibration, and it came in the form of light. Its purpose was to increase humanity's role in universal thought and participation. The time when it came and the results it left behind are significant. The work in this material is just a glimpse into the transformation taking place for all who inhabit this realm of supposed reality.

Why I received information about this event, I am not sure. The fact that I was somehow given additional information about what took place is also a mystery to me. What I do know is that the insights I have received have taken me on a journey I feel has just begun. The fact that I heard the name Tápu'at and realized that the design of a labyrinth was the beginning of our emergence to a higher realm of thought was not an accident. There are many different designs for labyrinths, but the one chosen was of Hopi origin, and the fact that I knew the name was also not a coincidence. The image of a labyrinth is highly symbolic. The interpretation by Frank Waters in his book that the labyrinth was seen and understood as an emergence (of mother and child) was the beginning of a journey for me that has expanded my consciousness. The labyrinth was not chosen at random but selected for the truth of its properties in relation to what mankind perceives as life's journey. The travels through the labyrinth are not like anything one thinks of as a life stream. One sees life in a sequence that appears orderly and as a natural progression. The labyrinth does not necessarily take on man's concept of life's journey through time and space. Mankind will learn that they are emerging into a realm of consciousness that requires not only their conscious participation but also an understanding that they are at the doorway of an adventure in what is perceived as change—not the continuation of current beliefs but a realignment of their roles that will seemingly no longer fit their prior concepts of reality.

The time of change is accelerating to match the light that is entering the conscious spectrum of third-dimensional thinking. The speeding up of time is an alignment of the space-time continuum. As I have stated several times, it appears to be the result of the December 2016 event that took place in the constellation of Cygnus. The event must have taken place many light-years prior to my receiving insight into the event. The exact location of this event is yet to be revealed for reasons that are not known by this writer.

What must take place is the result of changing conditions on the planet. These changes will require more cooperation and understanding and less intolerance and ignorance of the rules of life in relation to one another. The true nature of our reality is to bring forth harmony, not discord. The true nature of what life is meant to produce is an alignment with the greater aspect of humanity's qualities and not the perception of life that has been experienced for eons. The kill-or-be-killed aspect of this realm is the opposite of what love is. Mankind will, by the laws of creation, begin to understand that what was is no longer normal and acceptable. Mankind is reflective of an inner truth. The time of transition is here; his conscious thoughts and beliefs are to be raised, not through a forced application of consciousness and ideology but through a release of knowledge that allows each man, woman, and child an opportunity to consciously select the path of his or her journey in whichever direction it takes him or her.

The moment of time and the placement of space dictate that change is upon the present as never before. The release from old concepts of existence is a required ingredient in the current moment and beyond. This is the moment of expression. This moment is set in a scene that man has known from the beginning of his conscious travel through the third dimension. The way forward is to realize that the focus of what was, is, and will be is from the heart and not from the mind. Intelligence is a gift, but the gift has been misunderstood and, thus, misapplied throughout recorded history. The moment calls for greater reflection on how to move the dials of time and space seemingly forward. This work is a prelude to what comes next: a change in consciousness that is elevated not from intelligence or the mind but from the receptivity of the heart. That which is within the cave of the heart opens to a greater understanding of the future brought forward to the moment of self-realization.

The tools for the future are presented in this material in a fashion that appears on the surface to be part of the same dynamic of existing logic and reason. Nothing can be further from the truth.

The effort put into these exercises will yield over time a consistent train of consciousness that will allow for a purer understanding of the forms creation takes and the reasons for their presence. All of life is at once moving forward to a dynamic that is above the present horizon of conscious thought and awareness. This dynamic is revealed through conscious effort and purity of intent. Energy follows thought. What else does it follow? It follows the matrix of creation that is present. The illusion of time, space, and place is being altered, and mankind is being awakened to this reality.

The focus of this material has been to process this information in such a way that it does not jolt one's consciousness but awakens it to certain relevant facts that lead one to become more aware of his or her current state of mind and to find a more enlightened path out of the labyrinth of man's creation. The focus is on raising consciousness, not fear and doubt. The reality is that you can only remove obstacles in your path if you are aware of their existence.

Although this is the end of this material in written form, it is only the continuation of a process undertaken by many souls on Earth and in the celestial realms. The focus today should be on how we all improve ourselves and our connection to one another and the earth. We are an expression of creation, and as such, we have been given the light to move forward in a way that can provide harmony and unity without the rule of isolated thinking and beliefs. The light we have been given is open and available to all of mankind. Let us take this opportunity to realize that the gift we are is the gift of life. Peace.

Fourth Wisdom Stratum

Only speak words of wisdom when you are wise.

Wisdom is the insight to understand what is beyond the obvious.

Seek wisdom by going beyond the obvious.

The thought you are now thinking came from somewhere. Do you know its source?

Our Journey to Truth Continues

We are creating a series of workshops for those who want to explore deeper into the aspect of our higher nature and our relationship to the universe. We are part of the matrix of life and the covenant of creation. The challenge is: How do we move past our current perceptions of reality and open ourselves to the light that is within?

Our initial workshops will be "All About Core Consciousness – A Way to Elevated States of Awareness." We welcome you to connect with us on social media and be sure to sign up for emails on our website, wisdomstratum.com. Our website has information about upcoming workshops and new material that we are working on.

Appendixes

Appendix A

Definitions of Potential, Tápu'at, and Other

Potential

- The use of the power of imagination
- The freedom to act
- The ability to make of yourself something you can believe in
- The unlimited capacity to create
- The unwillingness to accept the status quo
- What comes next
- "Capability of being or becoming" (Webster's College Dictionary)
- "A latent excellence or ability that may or may not be developed" (Webster's College Dictionary)
- "The unlimited use of life's gifts" (what God would say)
- The unlocking of the confines of self as seen from within
- The truth manifested

Tápu'at

- The labyrinth of existence in this and future worlds
- The way forward out of the darkness of group consciousness

- The steps of the ancestors made anew by the light of a new day
- The emergence of conscious intent to be whole
- The fragments of ancient beliefs left behind by the dynamics of Earth's evolution
- The growth of human consciousness
- Evolution of humanity from darkness (lack of knowledge) to the light of true unity (knowledge expressed as truth)

Other

- Something outside the self
- Our shadow
- Promoter of separation
- Judgment made manifest
- A way to promote conflict
- The opposite of truth
- The smallness of man in manifestation
- The release of reality and true realization
- Incompleteness
- Creator of chaos, not harmony
- Light ignored

There is no other!

Appendix B

What Do We Know about Light?

Light has been with us since the beginning. The Bible states it was an integral part of our creation story. Over recorded time, we have added to our knowledge and gone through different levels of theories and experiments to come to the accepted knowledge of today. We know what light does for us in our homes, neighborhoods, and beyond. How it works is something that most of us take for granted unless we lose it for one reason or another.

The light of today is used in ways unimagined as recently as one hundred years ago. Over time, we have added terms like *speed of light* and *light-years*. One scientist, Stephen Hawking, has even suggested we will eventually be able to travel using beams of light. Einstein is quoted as saying, "For the rest of my life, I will reflect on what light is."

The following is a basic recap of what we currently know about light. It is not meant as a scientific discourse on the subject with formulas and charts, because I do not consider myself qualified to provide one.

Light is electromagnetic radiation. It is a wave that we can expand and radiate in all directions. It can carry energy and has momentum. It also interacts with matter and can flow through a vacuum.

Light's wave properties are amplitude, wave speed, wavelength, and frequency.

The amplitude of a light wave is a measurement of its intensity or brightness.

Because light waves are electromagnetic, there is a broad spectrum in how they interact with matter. The electromagnetic spectrum includes radio, microwave, infrared, visible light, ultraviolet, x-rays, and gamma rays.

Visible light makes up a narrow range of the light spectrum.

The frequency of a light wave is related to its color. White light is considered polychromatic. Monochromatic light is red, orange, yellow, green, blue, or violet. It is of note that these basic colors are central to the chakra system of ancient India.

The properties of light include the speed of light, reflection, superposition, refraction, wavelength, frequency, and color.

The speed of light in a vacuum is approximately 186,282 miles per second.

The bending of light rays when they pass through a surface between one transparent material and another is called refraction.

A light-year is a unit of length used to express astronomical distances.

All of the information above comes from various sources based on scientific study, experiments, and known facts. What has been accepted as fact has been done so over time. As time has gone by, we have added to our knowledge of light. The information in this book takes the subject of light in new directions. The results of this information will be up to mankind and how he processes and learns from the material. Over time, theories have been proven right, wrong, and then, with some modification, right again. The light of understanding is based on a willingness to allow knowledge and wisdom in. What we do with that knowledge leads us in a way that can create a better future for ourselves and others, or we can maintain our current set of beliefs that we presently experience. Light is available for us to learn and grow.

The mystery of and fascination with light have been with us since the beginning. There are origin stories and legends that cover most, if not all, of our ancient cultures. Writers, poets, artists, mystics, scientists, educators, and the merely curious across time have been absorbed and wondered at the various attributes of light.

The ancients used sunlight to create monuments, such as Stonehenge in England and Newgrange in Ireland, to mark the time of the seasons and to honor the gods. Ancient temples in Egypt also used the rays of the sun, welcoming their light and radiance, for ceremonies currently hidden by history. Our ancestors studied the light of the stars, developed calendars, and understood the celestial cycles in ways we can only marvel at today. The Antikythera mechanism from ancient Greece predicted astronomical positions and eclipses for calendar and astrological purposes. Whether it be the light of the sun or the light of the stars, we have responded to and will continue to respond to light as an integral part of who and what we are.

There are two lines from a bard's song in *All Things Are Lights* by Robert Shea that I have always remembered: *"One light outshines all lights above/The light within the light of love."*

Appendix C

Labyrinths

Webster's *College Dictionary* defines a labyrinth in the following ways:

> "A complicated irregular network of passages or paths in which it is difficult to find one's way; a maze".

> "A place constructed of or full of intricate passageways and blind alleys, a complex labyrinth of tunnels and chambers".

In truth, the labyrinth is not a maze. It has only one way in and one way out. It has been used for thousands of years as an archetype of our path of creation. The labyrinth has been used, and is still being used, as a tool or template for personal and spiritual growth.

One of the first labyrinths was found in Luzzanas, Sardinia, dating back to approximately 1500 to 1000 BCE. Another similar labyrinth was found in stone near Tintagel, England (ca. 1800 to 1400 BCE). The part that makes this of interest is that the design, which is known as a Cretan-style labyrinth, is nearly the exact same design as the Hopi labyrinth that gave me insight into the Emergence. The exact date of the Hopi labyrinth is not known, but it certainly wasn't three thousand years old.

A significant number of labyrinths both old and new can be found in caves, tombs, churches, and open spaces; on mountaintops; in people's front yards and backyards; and on the stone walls where ancient petroglyphs are found. They can be octagonal, round, or square. Most are seven or eleven circuits. Each circuit is an aspect of the path that you walk, run, or dance to the center and return to complete your journey.

When you see a labyrinth and choose to experience it, you will have two perspectives: (1) a pattern, which in most cases is a complete symmetrical design, and (2) the path you are choosing to walk, which leads you to the center in a rather circuitous manner. The vision seems to represent a meandering of sorts: order and disorder, or clarity and confusion.

For many, the labyrinth has a deep spiritual meaning. Those who feel a need to balance themselves or pray for guidance walk the path of a labyrinth in a meditative or contemplative manner. The ancients knew that these designs spoke to us in ways that could bring about healing and insight. Most labyrinths use sacred geometry to fulfill their objectives. When sacred geometry is used, there is a harmonic that resides within the pattern that can bring about changes within the person entering the labyrinth. Our consciousness has a pattern, or resonance. When we enter a sacred space, our consciousness can experience that which is of a higher frequency, which will assist us along the path we have chosen.

Walk the path of now, and understand what it takes to realize the sacred in each breath of life. Live life well, and live it in joy.

Part of this purpose seems to relate to what takes place when you walk a labyrinth. As you turn in a labyrinth, there is a shift. Sig Lonegren, in his *Labyrinths: Ancient Myths and Modern Uses*, refers to the *labys* and the turn as the pathway of truth. I have experienced this shift in my mind. It is like a mirror that switches position so that we may see things differently.

Jill Purce, in *The Mystic Spiral: Journey of the Soul*, wrote, "As the labyrinth creates and dissolves, expands and contracts, so it reveals and conceals. It is the cosmos to those who know the way, and chaos to those who lose it." She goes on to state, "For, as it is necessary to be born from the womb to see this world, only he who is born from himself sees the other world." The flow of one's path through the labyrinth of life is in finding one's higher self. The journey is of one's making, but it relates to all that is from the greater plan of the cosmos. We can emerge from the labyrinth of third-dimensional existence to receive that which is within, that which is truth. The question is, do you know the way?

There are many books written on the subject of labyrinths. I have included the names of several in the bibliography. They range from the construction to the spiritual aspects of labyrinths. Several books trace the labyrinth from the earliest recorded examples that have been found or written about to those that are currently in use.

Appendix D

Unexplained Mysteries of Earth and Beyond

Because of the tendency to doubt the introduction of different ideas and concepts, I have decided to list a few of the documented mysteries that cannot be explained based on our current level of knowledge.

Tabby's Star, or KIC 8462852

This is a star located in the constellation of Cygnus. It is approximately 1,280 light-years from Earth. Astronomers have observed that something is causing the brightness of the star to change over time. This dimming process is currently not understood by scientists. The star's brightness has been reduced by 15 to 22 percent on occasion. The exact cause is currently a mystery. This phenomenon is currently being studied by volunteers and scientists across the globe.

The Star That Should Not Exist

The star is called SDSS J102915+172927 and is located in the constellation of Leo. It is believed to be thirteen billion years old and made up of mostly hydrogen and helium elements. It is approximately

80 percent of the size of our sun. According to scientific simulations, this is considered too light to condense and form as a star. But nonetheless, there it is.

What Is Dark Matter?

It seems that scientists are able to observe only 5 percent of the stuff that makes up the universe. Depending on the source, approximately 80 percent of the universe is made up of material called dark matter, which we cannot directly observe. Because scientists cannot see dark matter, they have developed theories based on observations and studies to support their work. Another article I found indicated that dark matter made up approximately 27 percent, not 80 percent, of the universe.

What Is Dark Energy?

Based on the prior study, the universe is made up of approximately 68 percent dark energy. Scientists at one time thought the universe would slow down or stop expanding based on gravitational pull. When they studied the rate of expansion, they found that the universe was not only expanding but was doing so at a faster rate than they'd believed. They theorized that the universe is filled with a changing energy field. Albert Einstein, in his work, indicated that space was not empty.

The City of Nan Madol, near Micronesia

Archaeologists are unable to identify who built a city of approximately one hundred artificial islands made out of large basalt blocks. The technology and ability to build these islands did not supposedly exist from 200 BC to around AD 800. The islands are connected by viaducts. One article states that 250 million tons of basalt make up these islands. Why would the builders of these islands put such a vast quantity of basalt near a coral reef, but the bigger question is, How did they do it?

King Tut's Dagger

After years of study, a scientist determined that the dagger found in King Tut's tomb was made of a composition of metals that findings suggest came from a meteorite. How were the ancient Egyptians able to work with this material to produce such a blade, when that technology was supposedly not available to them?

The Dashka Stone

This stone was discovered in the village of Chandra in Bashkortostan, Russian Federation. It is believed to be approximately 120 million years old. This stone was studied by scientists at Bashkir State University. Their conclusion was that it came from an ancient civilization with high technical and cultural levels. Based on reports, the stone has some unusual characteristics:

- The first layer of the Dashka stone consists of eighteen centimeters of cement or ceramic based on dolomite.
- The second layer is made of diopside glass. It is approximately one inch thick and enriched with silicon, according to researchers, to provide picture strength.
- The third porcelain layer is several millimeters thick. According to scholars, this might have been placed in order to create diffused light to illuminate the stone slab but also to protect the slab from external impact thanks to its calcium-porcelain composition.

According to Alexander Nikolayevich Chuvyrov, a professor of physical and mathematical science, the stone was artificially made. The stone slab is also known as the Map of the Creator.

The surface of the stone slab is covered with a 3-D map of a portion of the Ural Mountains. It appears to be hand-carved, and the details of the area are amazingly accurate when seen from the above.

There are many other examples I could list, but the idea, as stated above, is to demonstrate that there are many things above Earth and on Earth that cannot be explained by scientific or rational means. Our consciousness accepts what appears real. The challenge for us is to go beyond our current level of consciousness to arrive at a level of awareness that fulfills our roles not only as inhabitants of this planet but also as an expression of the light the dwells within us.

Bibliography

Algeo, John. The Theosophical Labyrinth[Article]. - Los Angeles: Theosophy - June 3, 2012.

Allain, Rhett. 5 Things Every Human Should Know about Light [Online] // Wired.com. - February 11, 2015. - August 30, 2017. - www.wired.com.

Andrei, Mihai. ZME SCIENCE [Online]. - May 15, 2017. - August 25, 2017. - zmescience.com.

Artress, Lauren. Walking a Sacred Path [Book]. - New York: Rivehead Books, Division of G. P. Putnam and Sons, 1995.

Champion, Alex. Earth Maze [Book]. - Emeryville: Earth Maze Publishing, 1990.

Cooper, Keith. Kepler Finds Tabby's Star Is Mysteriously Dimming [Online] // Astronomy Now. - August 8, 2016. - August 26, 2017. - astronomynow.com.

Doob, Penelope Reed. The Idea of the Labyrinth [Book]. - New York: Cornell Paperbacks, 1992.

Elert, Glenn. The Physics Hybertext Book [Book]. - [s.l.]: physics. info, 1998-2017.

Gasdin-Cochrane, Marlene. The Mystery of King Tut's Dagger Solved with XRP [Online] // ThermoFisher Scientific. - July 19, 2016. - August 26, 2017. - thermofisher.com.

Giri Janavatar, Swami Sri Yukteswar. The Holy Science [Book]. - Los Angeles: Self-Realization Fellowship, 1990.

Green, Marian. The Path through the Labyrinth [Book]. - Dorset: Element Books Ltd, 1988.

Hall, Manley P. The Noble Eightfold Path [Book]. - Los Angeles: The Philosophical Research Society Inc., 1964.

Hawking, Stephen. Stephen Hawking Wants Humans to Reach Other Worlds via a Beam of Light // Stephen Hawking Wants Humans to Reach Other Worlds via a Beam of Light. - [s.l.]: NBC News, June 22, 2017.

Hawkins, David R. Power vs. Force: The Hidden Determinants of Human Behavior [Book]. - Carlsbad: Hay House, Inc, 2002.

Jaskolski, Helmet. The Labyrinth: Symbol of Fear, Rebirth, and Liberation [Book]. - Boston: Shambhala Publications Inc., 1997.

Jones, Roger A. Physics for the Rest of Us [Book]. - Chicago: Contemporary Books Inc., 1992.

Kern, Hermann. Through the Labyrinth: 5,000 Years of an Archetype [Book]. - New York: Prestel, 2000.

Levy, David H. Skywatching [Book]. - Berekley: The Nature Company, 1994.

Lonegren, Sig. Labyrinths: Ancient Myths and Modern Uses [Book]. - Glastonbury: Gothic Image Publications, 1991.

Matthews, W. H. Mazes and Labyrinths: Their History and Development [Book]. - New York: Dover Publishing, 1970.

Pennick, Nigel. Mazes and Labyrinths [Book]. - London: Robert Hace Ltd, 1990.

Pilgrim Friends of Peace. Peace Pilgrim [Book]. - Santa Fe: Friends of Peach Pilgrim and Ocean Tree Books, 1982.

Pruce, Jill. The Mystic Spiral: Journey of the Soul [Book]. - New Yrok: Thames and Hudson Inc, 1980.

Ramanan, S.V. Ramanic Blog [Online]. - October 18, 2016. - August 27, 2017. - Ancient Code.com.

Reed, Nola Taylor. What Is Dark Energy? [Online] // Space.com. - May 1, 2013. - August 25, 2017. - www.space.com.

Reed, Nola Taylor. What Is Dark Matter? [Online] // Space.com. - June 15, 2017. - August 25, 2017. - www.apace.com.

Scudder, Jullian. How Do We Know We Have the Speed of Light Correct? [Online] // Forbes.com. - April 5, 2017. - August 25, 2017. - www.forbes.com.

Shea, Robert. All Things Are Lights [Book]. - New York: Ballatine Books, 1986.

Thomas, Michael. Top Ten Unexplaineed Mysteries of the Stars [Online] // Listverse.com. - December 5, 2012. - August 25, 2017. - listverse.com.

Wikipedia. "Light" - August 26, 2017. -https://en.wikipedia.org/wiki/light.

Wikipedia. "Speed of Light" August 27, 2017. -https://en.wikipedia. org/wiki/speed of light.

Wall, Mike. Alien Megastructure? Tabby's Star Continues to Baffle Scientists [Online] // Space.com. - August 22, 2017. - August 26, 2017. - www.space.com.

Waters, Frank. Book of the Hopi [Book]. - New York: Penguin Books USA, Inc, 1963.

Watson, Bruce. A Radiant History from Creation to the Quantum Age Light [Book]. - New York: Bloomsbury Publishing PLC, 2016.

West, Melissa Gayle. Exploring the Labyrinth: A Guide for Healing and Spiritual Growth [Book]. - New York: Broadway Books, 2000.

About the Author

This is Howard A. Cooper's first book. He felt compelled to write this book because of an event he experienced in December 2016. Due to the insights gained by this event, which he referred to as *The Reveal Transit,* and subsequent events related to his experience, Howard realized that the magnitude of change we were experiencing was unique and of great importance. The book reflects the thoughts, insights and information he has received.

Howard has over 40 years of senior management experience in several industries in his career. He has been a Corporate Controller for a NYSE company and has held CFO positions for cosmetics and retail companies in Southern California. He also owned a turnaround consulting business dedicated to guiding companies through very difficult financial and structural challenges. Throughout his career he worked with people and companies to maximize their full potential.

Over the years, Howard has traveled to sacred and mystical sites in the United States, Europe and Egypt in his search of ancient knowledge and wisdom. Like so many he has been a seeker for greater meaning in life and how to bring out the best in himself and others.

This first book is an introduction to a level of greater understanding and knowledge that exists within each of us.

He and his wife, Peggy, reside in Henderson, NV

Printed in the United States
by Bookmasters

Printed in the United States
By Bookmasters